LET'S DISCOVER MATHEMATICS 5
WORLD OF MATHEMATICS
by L G Marsh
illustrated by Chris Hoggett
A & C BLACK Ltd · London

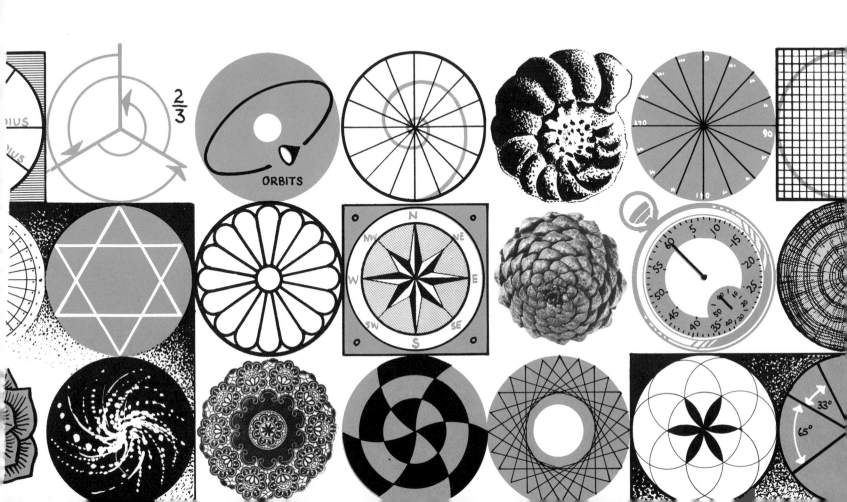

Contents

Grateful acknowledgement for permission to reproduce photographs is made to:
The National Monuments Register (page 20, Canterbury Cathedral);
A-Z Botanical Collections Ltd. (page 24, sunflower); United States Information Service (page 27, tornado);
The Rover Company Ltd. (page 91, Range Rover)

The LET'S DISCOVER MATHEMATICS series by L. G. Marsh

Let's Discover Shapes and Numbers—a beginning book
Let's Discover Mathematics Books 1–4
Answer books
Let's Discover Mathematics Book 5: WORLD OF MATHEMATICS
Workshops 1–3—sets of cards

Exploring the Metric System—including decimal currency
Exploring the Metric World
Answer books

Books for teachers by L. G. Marsh

Approach to Mathematics— *a study of groups of seven-year-old children exploring mathematical apparatus*
Alongside the Child in the Primary School

FIRST PUBLISHED 1972
ISBN 0 7136 1278 9
© 1972 A & C BLACK LTD   4, 5 & 6 SOHO SQUARE   LONDON W1V 6AD
PRINTED IN GREAT BRITAIN BY SIR JOSEPH CAUSTON & SONS LTD   LONDON & EASTLEIGH

Circles

Why?

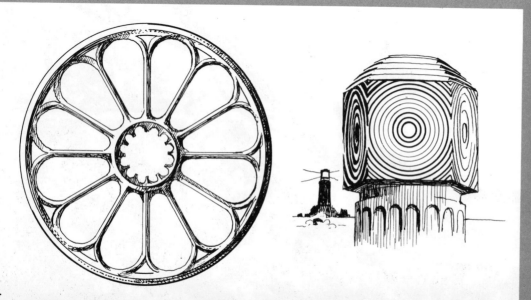

Round dances

Russian folk dance

The Maypole dance

Direction

Natural structure

Packing for storage

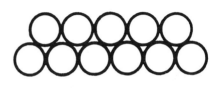

Circles

We see circles everywhere.

Make a record of any examples of circles you find.

Use your reference books to find examples of dances that use a circle as their main pattern.

The Maypole dance is one but there are many others. Make up some movement patterns of your own that are based on a circle. A group of people will enable you to work out some interesting patterns.

Make up a collection of photographs and drawings of circles. You can cut out from magazines and catalogues pictures of wheels, bottles, tins and other circular objects.

What do you notice about these circles? What are they used for?

What do you notice about these circles? What do they need to do?

Making patterns

A packet of coloured circle shapes can be folded and cut to make the patterns on this page. If you wish, you can cut out your own circle shapes.

This pattern can be made by overlapping circles. Make sure that you get the same overlap with each circle.

Using compasses to make patterns

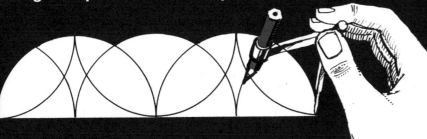

Drawing circles

Mark a point in the middle of a piece of paper. Call this point C. Now draw as many points as possible that are 5cm from C. Try to surround C with points. The drawing on this page only shows the beginning. What do you notice about the points you have drawn?

Join each of the points to its neighbouring point. What shape (roughly) have you drawn?

°C

This is another way to draw a circle.

Try drawing several sizes of circle. What do you have to change in order to alter the size of the circle?

Make a large circle in your playground, using a long rope, a piece of chalk and a post.

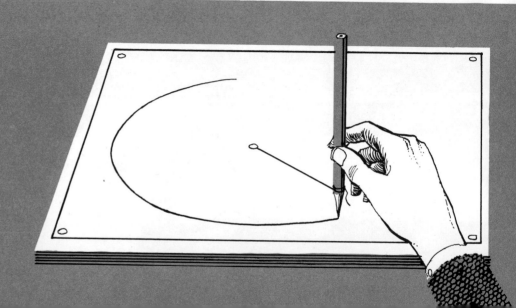

Another way to draw a circle.

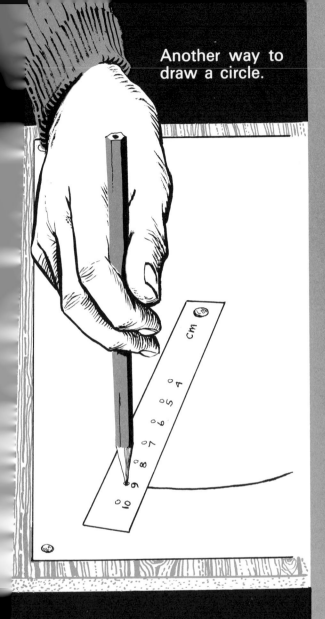

Use a narrow strip of card with holes for the pencil point from 4 to 10cm. Fix a drawing pin at O, put a pencil point through one of the holes and make a circle.

Use a strip of thin card and mark on the edge three points: A, B and C, which should be equally spaced.

Make a mark in the centre of a sheet of paper and call it M. Place your card strip so that point B touches point M.

Mark dots at A and C.

Keep moving the card strip around a little at a time and always keeping point B on M until you have made a circle of dots. Then join up the dots.

When drawing circles what have you noticed about the distance of each dot on the circumference from the centre of the circle?

Using compasses

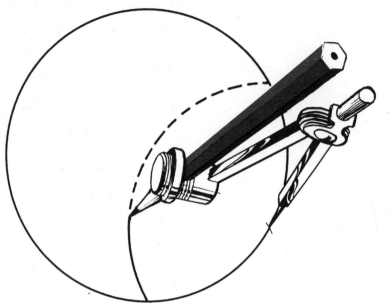

Draw a circle and keep the compasses with the same radius. Place the compasses on the circumference and draw your first segment of the same circle.

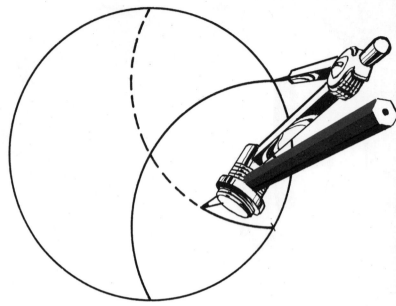

Continue moving the compasses around the circle to make six divisions with intersection points on the circumference.

Here we have the circumference divided by six again. The six intersection points along the circumference are joined to form a regular hexagon. By connecting every point on the circumference with the second one following it in either direction, you have a stellar hexagon.

Can you find two equilateral triangles in the circle?

Stellar hexagon

What do you notice about the central shape of this hexagon?

Make your own second drawing a regular hexagon and try to repeat the regular hexagon within your design.

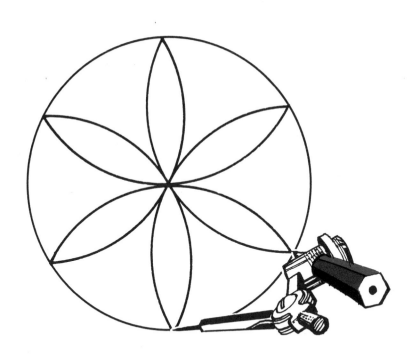

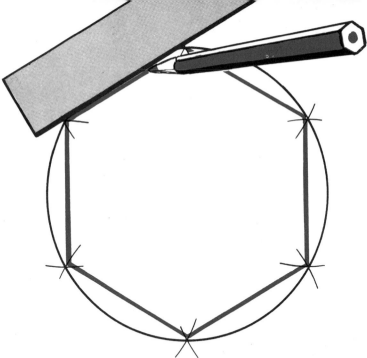

Here is the completed drawing. Use it to check your own work.

Here we have used the intersection points to draw a regular hexagon. Make a regular hexagon of your own, using the diagram to check your own work.

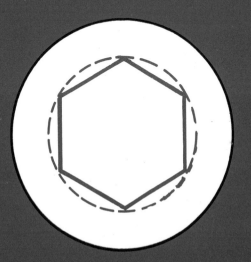

Arranging pennies

The centres of the pennies form the vertices of a regular hexagon and their radii are one half of the length of the hexagon sides.

Arrange six pennies around a seventh penny.

Try to make your own drawing of this pattern of pennies.

Making circles

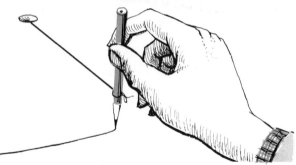

As you move your string around the centre to draw a circle, the string makes the radius of the circle.

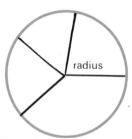

Each line in the diagram is called a radius. More than one are called radii.
What do you notice about the length of each radius?

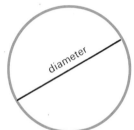

If you draw a straight line through the centre of the circle from one point on the circumference to another point on the circumference, how much bigger than the radius is the diameter?

Folding circles

Draw round a coin and cut out the circle. Make a set of circles for the experiments on this page.

Fold the paper in half.

Open the folded circle and draw along the line of the fold.
This line is called a diameter.

Take your circle and fold it in half.

Fold it again. Each of these straight edges is called a radius.

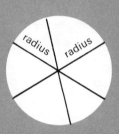

Each fold is like the spoke of a wheel.

12

Measuring

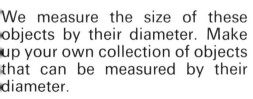

We measure the size of these objects by their diameter. Make up your own collection of objects that can be measured by their diameter.

1 graph paper and wooden blocks

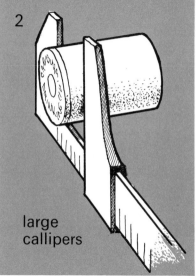

2 large callipers

3 tape measure

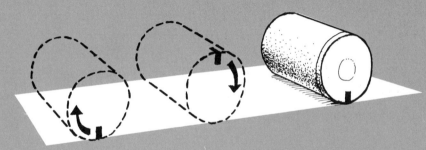

4 Make a mark on a tin and roll it along a strip of paper so that it makes a full turn. Measure the distance between starting point and finishing point.

5 Wind a thin strip of paper round a tin. Use a pin to prick through where the strip overlaps.
Open out and measure between the two pinpricks.
The measurement is the circumference of the tin.

Object	Diameter	Circumference
saucer		
cocoa tin		
table mat		

Keep a record of your measurements. Keep this tabulation because you will need it later.

Measuring circles

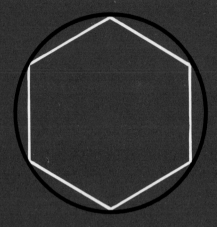

Draw a circle and a regular hexagon inside it.

What do we know about the length of the radius of a circle and each side of a hexagon constructed within it?

Which is larger—the circumference of a circle or the circumference of the hexagon?

How many times does the radius fit into the hexagon?

How many times does the diameter fit into the circumference of the hexagon?

Is the circumference of the circle longer or shorter than 3 diameters?

Draw a square so that each side touches the circumference of the circle.

What do you notice about the length of the diameter of the circle and the length of each side of the square?

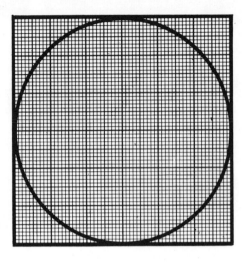

Find the circumference of the square and the circle. Which is longer?

How many times does the diameter fit into the circumference of the square?

Is the circumference of the circle shorter or longer than 4 diameters?

Is the circumference nearer in length to the 3 diameters, as in the hexagon, or to the 4 diameters as in the square?

Use a piece of string to measure the diameter of a circle and another piece to measure the circumference.

Divide the length of the circumference string by the length of the diameter string.

Try this for several circles. What do you notice about your pattern of answers?

Place small circular objects on your graph so that the diameters lie along the horizontal axis. Shade in a column (or stick down the length of string) to show the circumference of each circle.

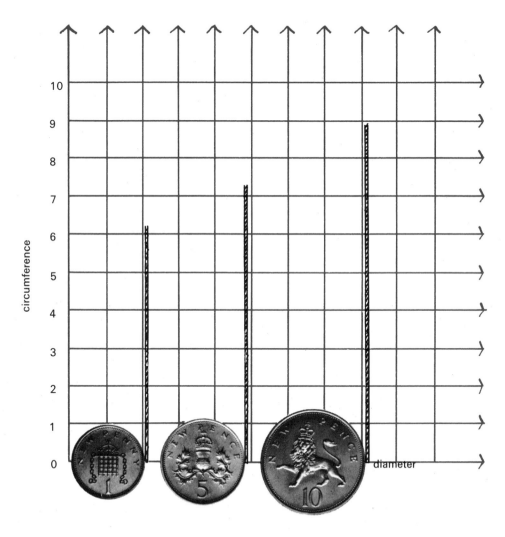

Use a felt-tip pen to draw on the same sheet of paper the 3 times table. What do you notice?

Make up your own illustrated account of the investigations on this page.

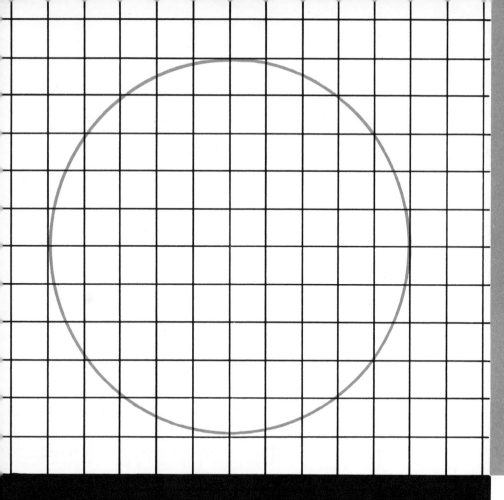

We can find the area of the circle by counting the units—in this case squares. We can make the task of counting the squares easier by drawing larger squares and rectangles.

Another way is to count the squares in one quarter and then multiply by four.

There is another way of finding the area of a circle.
Shade one half of a circle like this:

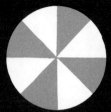

Fold the circle into eighths and cut along the folds.

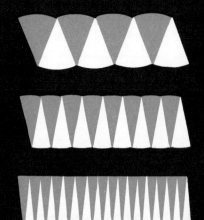

The separate pieces can be arranged to be, roughly, a parallelogram, with one side equal to the radius of the circle and the other equal to half the circumference of the circle.

The more sectors we have the nearer we get to a parallelogram.

So far we have:

1 found the area of circles by counting squares;

2 found the area by cutting the circle to make a parallelogram;

3 found a special relationship between the circumference and diameter of circles.

This special ratio is called after a letter of the Greek alphabet, π (pi). The value of π is roughly $3\frac{1}{7}$. Using decimals, we generally record it as $\pi = 3 \cdot 14$.

Knowing about the ratio of the circumference and the diameter means that we can find the circumference of any circle provided that we know its diameter.

Circumference $= \pi \times$ Diameter

Find the circumference of circles whose diameters are:

1 3cm **2** 5cm **3** 10cm

This is a circle divided into 64 sectors. You can make your own circle and cut out the sectors, arranging them to make a shape which is almost a rectangle, like the diagram on the right.

Finding the area without counting

Using our discoveries about the ratio π we can find the area of any circle without having to count squares.

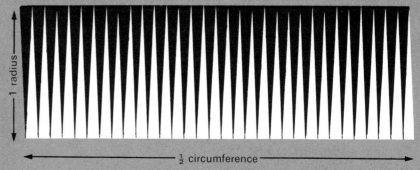

1 radius

½ circumference

The breadth of the rectangle is made up from 1 radius, the length is half the circumference (distance all round) of the circle. The circumference equals $\pi \times d$, so half the circumference is $\pi \times r$. So the area of the rectangle (and the area of the circle that was used to make the rectangle) is $\pi r \times r$ or πr^2.

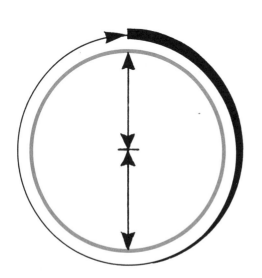

So we can find the area of a circle by multiplying $r \times r \times \pi$.

We usually write this as:

$= \pi r^2$

Investigate this idea and make up your own table.

Radius, cm	1	2	3	4	5	6	7	8	9	10
Area, cm²	$\pi \times 1$	$\pi \times 4$	$\pi \times 9$							

Patterns

Can you see how to make the pattern?

Trace over the pattern and fix a pin at A.

Turn the shape.

What do you notice?

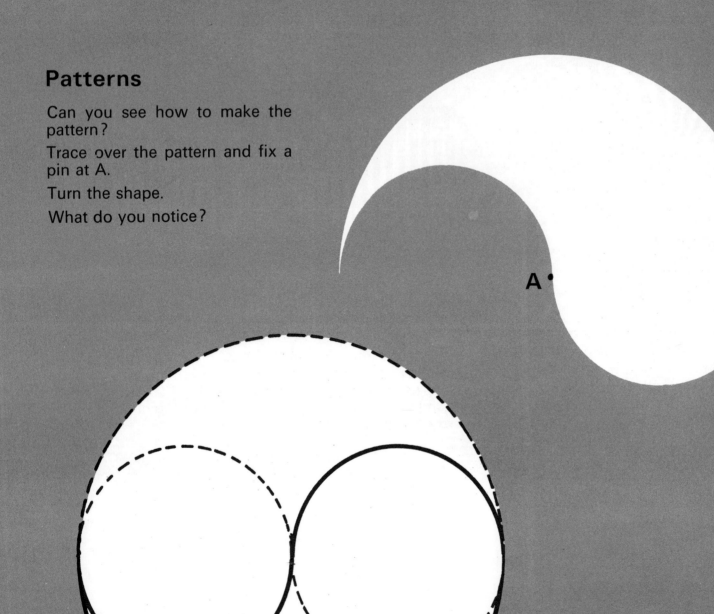

The pattern is constructed from three circles: two identical ones touching each other, both drawn inside a third circle which has double their radius.

If you draw two more of the larger circles so that each circle passes through the centre of the first larger circle, we begin a progressive pattern.

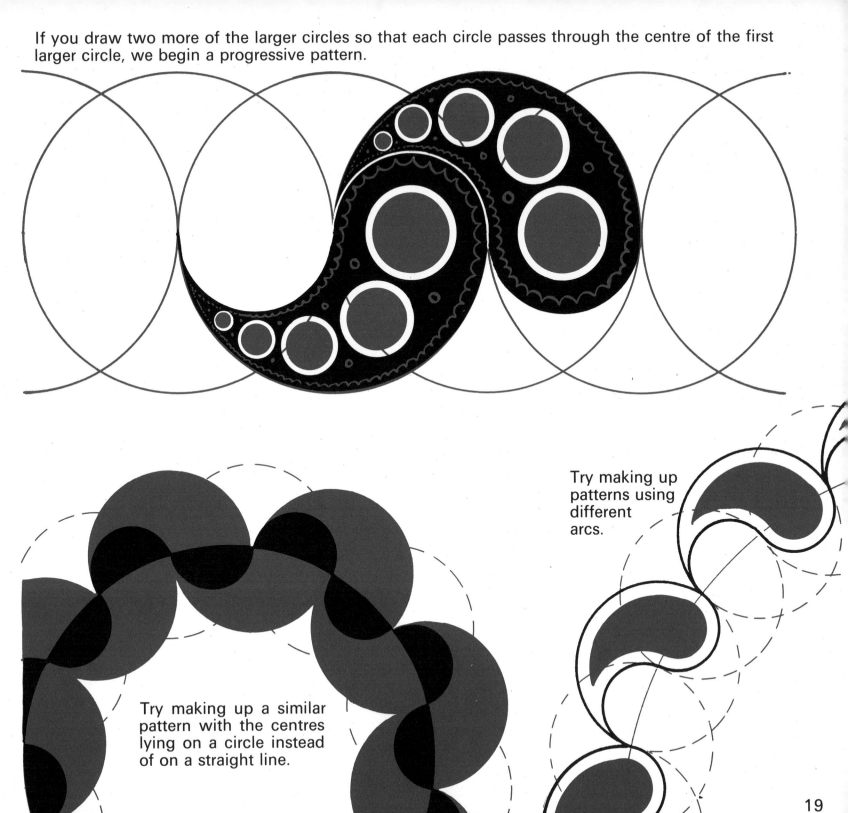

Try making up patterns using different arcs.

Try making up a similar pattern with the centres lying on a circle instead of on a straight line.

Patterns

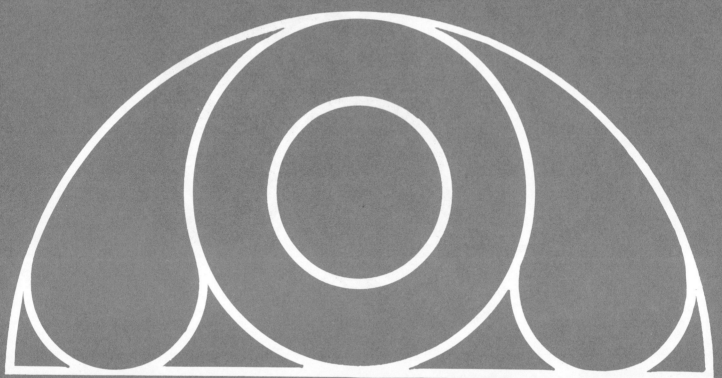

A diagram of a fanlight pattern. Many fanlights use rays and arcs, but try to find one that uses the full circle.

Look around for other patterns that use circles:

20 Rose window, Canterbury Cathedral

A paper doyley

A coal-hole cover

1

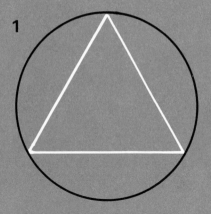

circle with
equilateral triangle
drawn inside

2

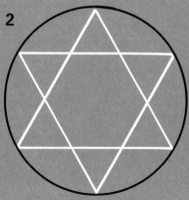

circle with
stellar hexagon
drawn inside

3

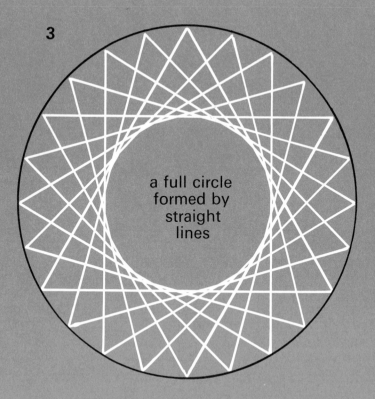

a full circle
formed by
straight
lines

It is possible to make these patterns with coloured threads 'stretched' on to thin card; or with string wound round pegs stuck in the ground.

A curve constructed in this way is called an envelope.

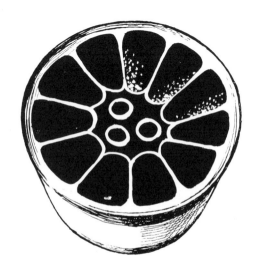

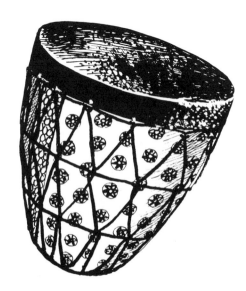

circle design on drums

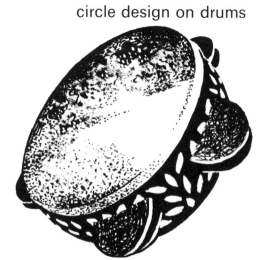

21

Ellipses

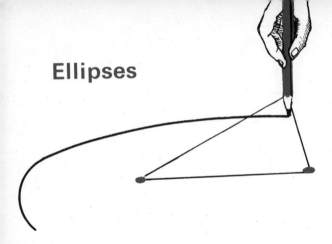

Use a length of string about 40cm long and form a loop with it. Fix the loop round two pins and stretch the string with your pencil. Keep the string tight and move the pencil round.

Try drawing several ellipses with the pins placed closer together and further apart.

If you have circular lampshades in your classroom, look at the shape made by the bottom edge. Move nearer the shade and then further away from it. What shape does the bottom edge seem to be?

Try looking at other circular objects from an angle.

Try tilting a glass of water—without spilling it! What do you notice?

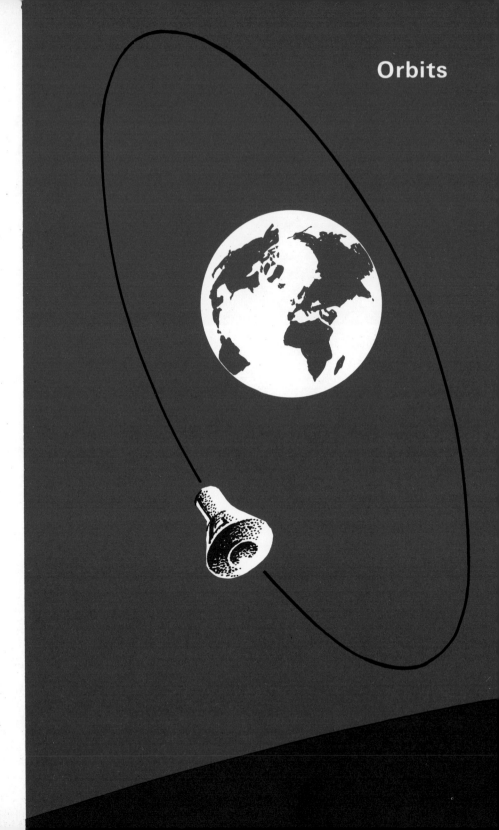

Distances from the Sun:

Mercury	58 million km	Jupiter	777 million km
Venus	108 million km	Saturn	1426 million km
Earth	150 million km	Uranus	2869 million km
Mars	228 million km	Neptune	4495 million km
		Pluto	5900 million km

The Earth moves round the Sun in an orbit which is in the shape of an ellipse. The Moon moves round the Earth making the same elliptical orbit. When a spacecraft is launched it goes 'into orbit' round the Earth and again this traces out an elliptical shape.

Circles and spirals

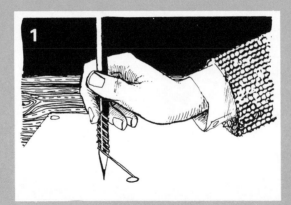

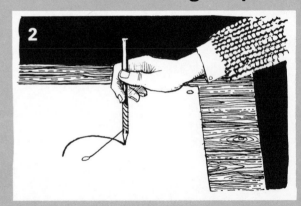

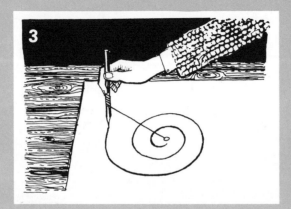

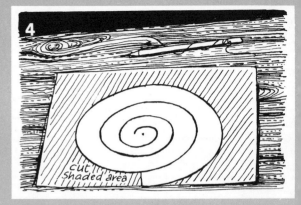

A spiral is a flat or plane shape. Draw a spiral on a piece of paper or card and cut along the spiral track with a pair of scissors.

1 Cut along the spiral track.

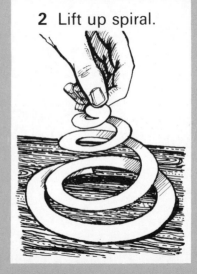

2 Lift up spiral.

3 What do you notice about this shape?

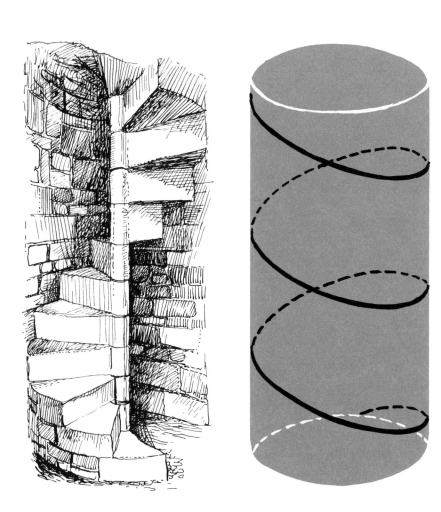

a spiral staircase	a cylindrical helix
a helter-skelter	a conical helix
a circus globe	a spherical helix

We talk about spiral staircases but in fact the correct name for a spiral staircase is a *helix*. Mathematically it is correct to call a shape a spiral when it is a flat or plane shape. When it is three-dimensional it is called a helix. It is like a spiral drawn on a cylinder. It is possible to draw a helix on a cylinder, a cone or even a sphere.

Try coiling a length of thick string so as to give a bird's eye view of a winding staircase and a helter-skelter.

Finding examples

If at all possible, collect actual examples of spirals and helices. Bedsprings, bolts, etc. will be easy to find but you will have to make do with photographs or drawings of tornadoes!

a plan view of a whelk   an ammonite   an aerial view of a tornado

Drawing a spiral

There are different kinds of spirals. On this page we learn how to draw the spiral named after the Greek scientist, Archimedes.

Cut out a large circle and fold it to give you 16 divisions.

1

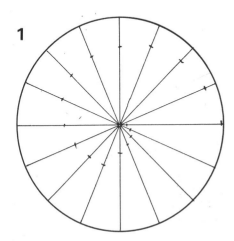

2

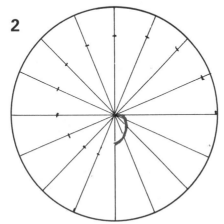

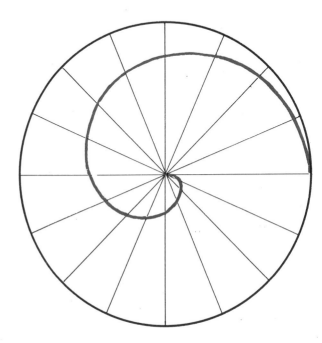

Choose a length for a step and then move from radius to radius in equal steps. In the diagram the steps are marked in.

Carry on joining up each step on your own diagram.

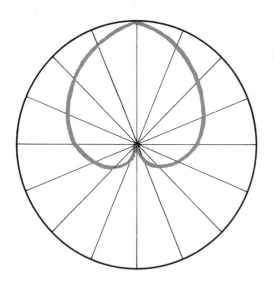

More spirals

Here is a drawing of two Archimedes' Spirals. They start from the same point to the right and to the left. The length of the steps has to be adjusted if the radius is to be used up after the number of steps in half a circle.

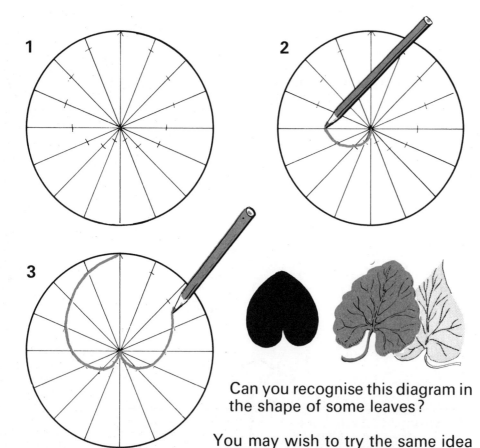

1

2

3

Can you recognise this diagram in the shape of some leaves?

You may wish to try the same idea using an equilateral triangle.

The Logarithmic Spiral

Another spiral is the Logarithmic Spiral. Its shape is the result of growth and produces a curve that we often see in Nature.

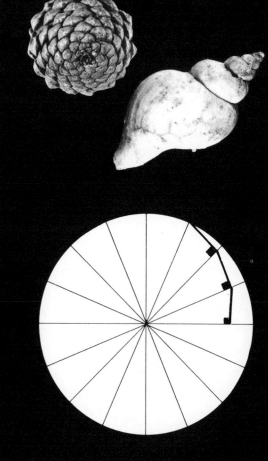

4 From this point drop a second perpendicular, and continue in the same way.

Making the Spiral

1 Draw a circle.

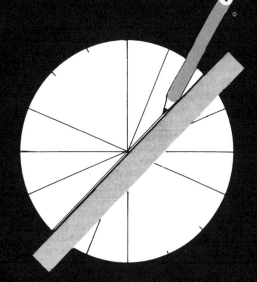

2 Divide the circle into **16** equal parts and draw in the radii.

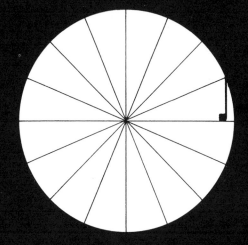

3 Drop a perpendicular from the starting point to the next radius.

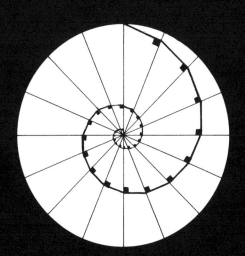

5 Perpendiculars drawn in.

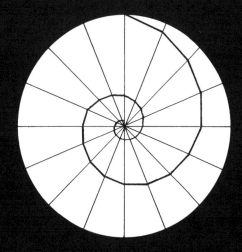

6 Completed.

7 The curve shown without construction lines.

Making patterns

1 Stitch a spiral shape on a piece of material, using a strong piece of wool or string.

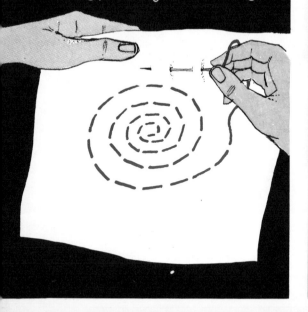

string.

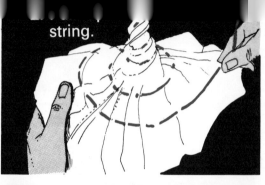

3 Tighter string and wind round base.

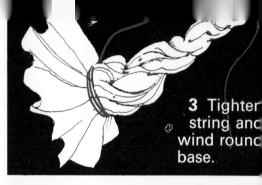

4 Dip into a small basin of dye for about five seconds.

5 Open out and hang up to dry.

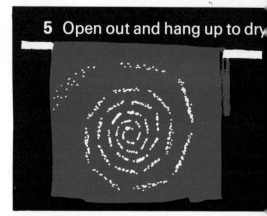

String printing

Object printing

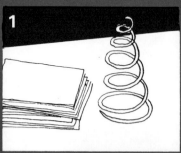

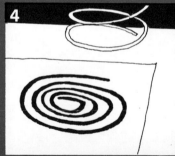

30

A useful helix

The distance between two threads of a screw or bolt is called the pitch. It is the distance that the bolt moves forward (or the nut on the bolt) when we give it one turn.

Find some bolts and measure their pitches.

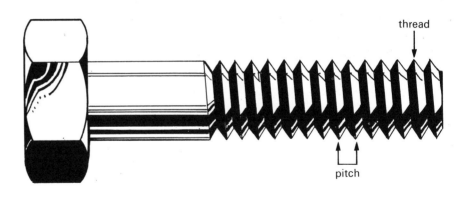

thread

pitch

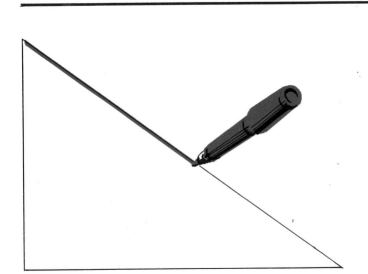

1 Cut out a paper right-angled triangle and mark the sloping edge with a felt-tip pen.

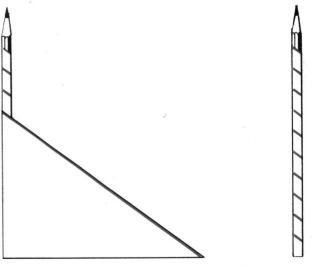

2 Wind the triangle round a pencil.

3 Completed spiral.

Make up spirals using cut-out triangles of different dimensions.

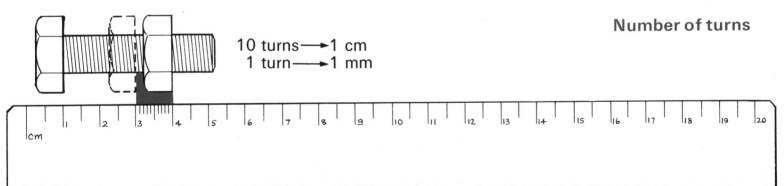

Number of turns

10 turns ➔ 1 cm
1 turn ➔ 1 mm

31

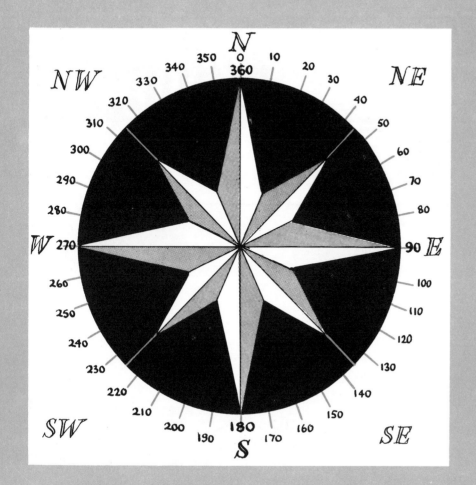

Directions and angles

When we mark off a compass card in degrees we see that there are 360 degrees in a complete turn.

Today various people are suggesting that we should use other units for measuring angles, but it is likely that we shall continue to use degrees as units for many years to come.

The Ancient Egyptians and Babylonians believed that the Sun moved round the Earth, taking one year of 360 days to cover the circular track. It is because of this that we have the idea that a full turn or circle has 360 degrees.

Look at the compass card.

Record the number of degrees in a turn from:

1 North to East   4 North to South-East
2 East to South   5 East to South-West
3 South to West   6 East to West
                        7 North to West

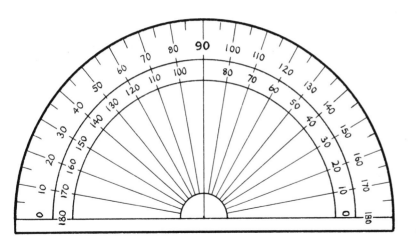

Angles

We use a protractor to discover that the angle is one of 50 degrees.

 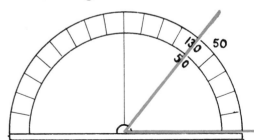

Use your protractor to measure these angles. They form a set of acute angles: { □°, □°, □°, □°, □° }

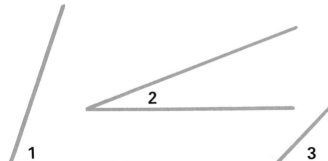 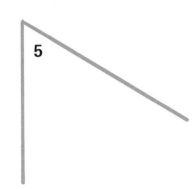

Use your protractor to measure these angles. They form a set of obtuse angles: { □°, □°, □°, □° }

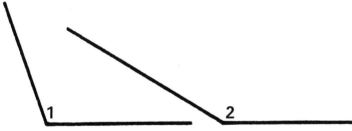 

33

Counting a class of children

 Graham

 Susan

 Don

 Alison

 Mary

 John

 Fred

 Yasmin

 Karen

 Carol

 David

 Andrew

 Margaret

 Michael

 Adam

 Charles

 Ian

 Ann

 Paul

 Juliet

 Peter

How many children?
How many boys?
How many girls?
How many children with books?
How many boys with short socks?
How many girls with short socks?
How many children with short socks?

How many children with glasses?
How many in the set of children?
How many in each of the two sub-sets of children?
Record the names of the sub-set of girls:
{Mary, Alison, □, □, □, □, □, □, □.}

Is this true:
{Fred, Margaret, Don, Graham, Charles} a sub-set of boys?
If it is not true, what sub-set is it?

Try to discover as much as possible about the set of children on this page and record your discoveries.

Sorting into sets and sub-sets

{cars} is the way we can record the diagram of the cars. The curly brackets stand for 'the set of'.

We read {cars} as 'the set of cars'.

{brown cars} ⊂ {cars}

In the diagram we have drawn in a line to show the sub-sets. To save writing 'is a sub-set of' we use the symbol ⊂.

We read {brown cars} ⊂ {cars} as 'brown cars is the sub-set of cars'.

Make up your own diagrams to show the sets and sub-sets and record your diagrams using curly brackets and the symbol ⊂.

More sorting

zebra   camel   tiger

. . . . . belong to the set of 'animals'

So that we do not have to write this in full, we can use to stand for 'belongs to' or 'is a member of'

It is similar in shape to the capital letter $\in$ in the word *Element*. We use capital letters to denote sets and small letters to denote the elements or members of the sets.

If A is the set of even numbers we can record: $2 \in A$, $4 \in A$, $6 \in A$.

Look at these diagrams:

1

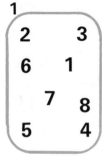

2   3
6   1
  7   8
5   4

What can we say about them?
1, 3, 7 and 5 are odd numbers less than 9.
2, 4, 6 and 8 are even numbers less than 10.
1, 2, 3, 4, 5, 6, 7 and 8 are counting numbers less than 9.

2

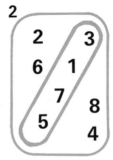

We can record our investigations like this:

$B = \begin{vmatrix} \text{odd numbers} \\ \text{less than 9} \end{vmatrix}$ or $B = \{1, 3, 7, 5\}$

$A = \begin{vmatrix} \text{even numbers} \\ \text{less than 10} \end{vmatrix}$ or $A = \{2, 4, 6, 8\}$

$N = \begin{vmatrix} \text{counting numbers} \\ \text{less than 9} \end{vmatrix}$

or $N = \{1, 2, 3, 4, 5, 6, 7, 8\}$

We have a special name for sets which are part of a larger set; they are called *sub-sets*. **B** is a sub-set of **N**.

All the numbers in **N** are members of the set of counting numbers less than 9. Another name for this set of numbers would be Natural Numbers. To save writing 'is a sub-set of' you can use the symbol ⊂.

Use the symbol ⊂ to make up your own examples of sets and sub-sets. Record the sets and sub-sets in these pictures:

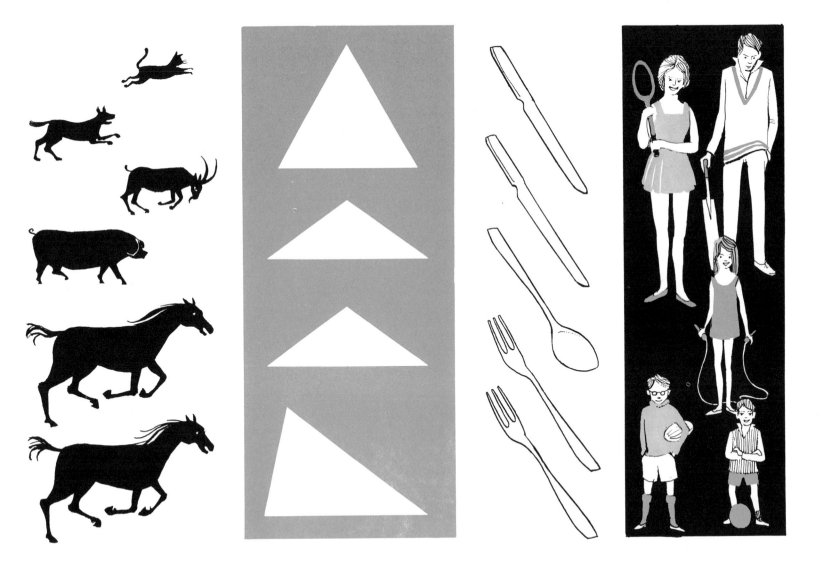

Months of the year

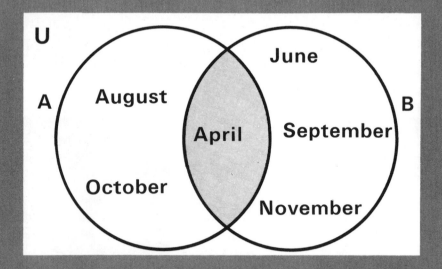

The diagram on this page is called a Venn diagram (after John Venn, an English mathematician who lived from 1834 to 1923). We can use this type of diagram to show sets. All the sets that are possibles for us to consider when we investigate the months in a year make up what is called the Universal Set. We have used **U** and the rectangle for this. Set **A** is the months of the year whose names begin with a vowel; Set **B** is the months of the year which have only 30 days.

Use the diagram to list the elements of these sets:
A = {months of the year whose names begin with a vowel}
B = {months of the year which have only 30 days}

A and **B** are sub-sets of **U** and we can make a third set from the intersection (the shaded part of the diagram) of **A** and **B**. So that we do not have to write the word 'intersection' or 'overlap' we use the symbol ∩.

We read **A** ∩ **B** as 'the intersection of sets **A** and **B**'.

Collections and sets

We have learnt about some of the symbols that we can use to describe our work with sets. When we count we decide which objects we shall include in our count; this makes up the elements of the set. We generally use capital letters to name a set and small letters to name the elements (members) of the set.

Another way of helping us to think about the word 'set' is to think of the word 'collection'.

1 Make up examples of collections of objects that could form a set.

2 Use the information in this book to make up your own examples of sets and sub-sets. Make sure you use the various symbols to describe sets as well as Venn diagrams.

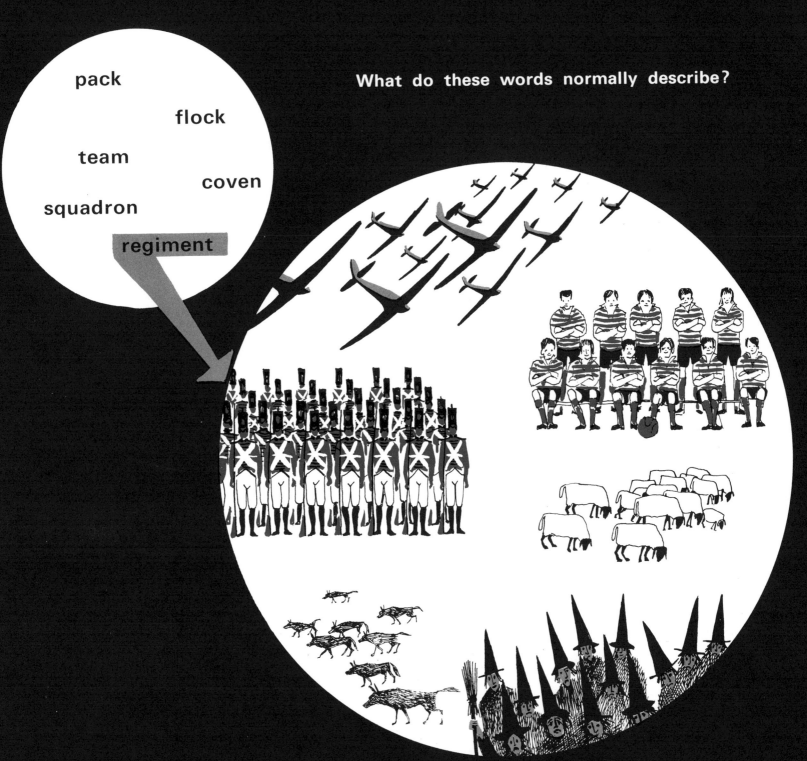

pack

flock

team

coven

squadron

regiment

What do these words normally describe?

Counting

Look at this picture and try to answer the question 'How many?' Do not use numerals to answer the question but think up you own ways of 'keeping the score' by using diagrams and pictures.

Matching

Men have used written numbers for about seven thousand years. Of course, the first ways of writing numbers did not use the same Arabic numerals that we use today.

Early Man could not count as we can, for he had no words to stand for numbers. If he had several animal skins he could not count them in order to find out whether he had one for each member of the family. Instead, he found out whether he had enough by giving a skin to his wife and one to each of his children. This is called *matching*.

In the same way we often match objects to people. If Mother wants to boil an egg for each person, how can she make sure that each person gets an egg—without counting or using number names?

When Mother wants to give a boiled egg to each person she matches the set of eggs to the set of people.

We describe the process of matching the elements of one set with the elements of another set as making a ONE-TO-ONE-CORRESPONDENCE. In this case it does not matter which person receives a particular egg, but it is important for each person to be matched with one egg!

Matching

a

b

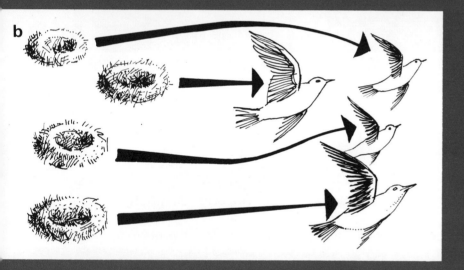

c

d

When we can set up a one-to-one-correspondence between the elements of two sets, we can say that the sets have the same CARDINAL NUMBER. Cardinal Numbers are used to describe sets of objects. Use Cardinal Numbers, 'set language' and Venn Diagrams to describe the drawings on this page.

e

'second' shepherd   'first' shepherd

Shepherds counting

A shepherd was counting sheep and using his fingers as a tally. If he matched one finger to each sheep he was able to count to ten. When he reached ten, the second shepherd raised one of his fingers and the first shepherd began counting again.

Look at the picture:

1 How many sheep have the shepherds counted?

2 How many sheep (using the method described) are the two shepherds able to count?

3 How many sheep could three shepherds count?

Shepherds counting sheep		Number of sheep counted
Number of fingers raised by the second shepherd	Number of fingers raised by the first shepherd	
	1 2 3 4	1 2 3 4 . . . . .
1	1	11

Make up your own table of sheep counting.

Counting

When we look at this picture there is no need to count. We can recognise that 'it is four' at one glance.

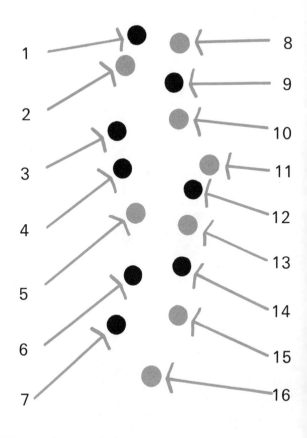

1
2
3
4
5
6
7

8
9
10
11
12
13
14
15
16

But when we look at the picture on the right we need to use our knowledge of counting. We make a one-to-one-correspondence between our number names and the objects.

When we have larger numbers and need to extend our number names, we make a pattern. We call this our *Number System*. We group one ten (ten), two tens (twenty), three tens (thirty) and so on . . .

one ten   two tens   three tens   four tens

0   10   20   30   40   50

44

Counting

When we count we agree to use number names in an accepted order and we think of the size of the collection by the number name we use for the last object.

Count the number of ducks on this page. When we say forty-eight, we are naming the forty-eighth duck, and using it to describe the fact that there are forty-eight ducks in the collection.

What is happening here?

one, two, three, four, five, six, seven, eight, nine, ten, eleven, twelve, thirteen, fourteen, fifteen, sixteen, seventeen, eighteen, nineteen, hifty, nifty, snifty, wifty, wem, hem, tem, fem, pem, zem, nem, imm, fimm, nimm, wiz, tiz, fiz, hiz, liz, biz, diz, kiz . . . hundred

Just imagine what would happen if, when we needed to count to one hundred, we had to use a hundred different and unrelated names. Many would find it impossible to remember all the names.

Fortunately, when we count we use number words that are in a pattern:
twenty-four stands for two *tens* and four units
thirty-four stands for three *tens* and four units
forty-four stands for four *tens* and four units

Our counting system uses what is called the collective unit. It works in the same way as the shepherds use when counting their sheep on page 43. The collective unit is based on ten—probably because we have ten fingers. Our decimal abacus and calculating machines have the first column for units, the second for tens, the third for hundreds, and so on.

But there are other collective units. There is a counting system based on five. David Smeltzer writes about the Joloffs of Africa whose first ten number words were:

1 wean	3 yat	5 judom	7 judom yar $(5 + 2)$	9 judom yanet $(5+4)$
2 yar	4 yanet	6 judom wean $(5 + 1)$	8 judom yat $(5 + 3)$	10 fook

Find out about various counting systems (see pages 17–25 of *Man and Number* by David Smeltzer, published by A & C Black).

Make up your own counting system.

Recording numbers

Egyptian numeral
for 10

Greek numeral
for 10

Chinese numeral
for 10

Babylonian
numeral for 10

See what you can discover about the various numeral systems and try one or two simple calculations in each system. Book 4 of *Let's Discover Mathematics* (pages 10–13) will help you.

Of all the earlier systems the Roman is one of the easiest to understand because we can see how the numerals used were based on finger counting.

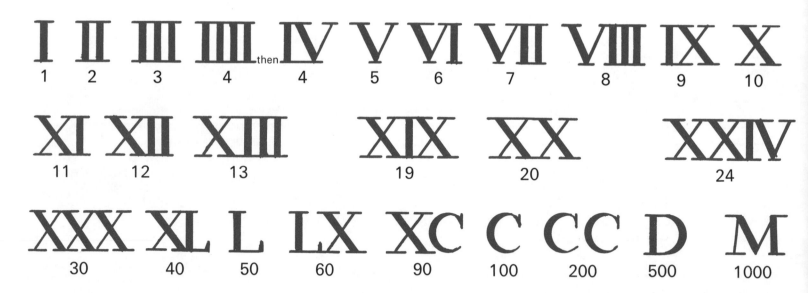

David Smeltzer in *Man and Number* (page 48) explains how the symbols were developed. Notice that I placed in front of V means 'subtract 1 from 5'.

When placed after V it means 'add 1 to 5'. In the same way, X before L means 'subtract 10' and X after L means 'add 10'.

A Record these in our system of numerals:

¹ **XXVII**   ² **XXXV**   ³ **XXIII**   ⁴ **XXIV**

⁵ **C**   ⁶ **CX**   ⁷ **CXV**   ⁸ **CXIV**   ⁹ **D**

¹⁰ **MLXVI**   ¹¹ **CDXLIV**   ¹² **LV**   ¹³ **MI**

B 1 Write this year's date in Roman numerals.

2 Record the year of publication of this book in Roman numerals.

C Try these multiplication sums:

¹ **LXI**
   V
────────

² **LXVII**
   XLII
────────

³ **MCV**
   LI
────────

Make up your own booklet about counting and recording. Notches on sticks or even pebbles will do to show one-to-one-correspondence, but after about six objects it becomes difficult to see the total at a glance. Because of this many early Number Systems had special marks for four or five. We group in tens and this makes it easier to answer the question:
'How many?'

Find out about various number systems and the words used for, say, ten in various languages. You will need to use your library books to help you with your investigations.

Our number system

You already know that in the twelfth century the Arabs were able to record any number in the world by using the nine different symbols 1 2 3 4 5 6 7 8 9 together with the secret sign, cypher or zero, 0.

Our system of numeration is based on groupings of tens and this is what we mean when we say that ten is the BASE of our number system.

Unlike the Romans we do not need to invent new symbols for hundreds, thousands and millions. The value of any numeral depends upon its position or place. Our system has place value for its numerals: in the number 271 the 7 is 'worth' 7 tens because of its place in the tens position. On an abacus it is easy to see the 'value' of each numeral.

It is easy to record the first abacus number—123; but with **b** 1 3 it is difficult to be sure of their values.

It is in such examples that we need to use the Arabic secret sign or 'cypher' (cypher is Arabic for empty space). We use zero, 0, to show this:

$$100 = 10 \times 10 \qquad \text{(ten tens are one hundred)}$$
$$= 10^2 \qquad \text{('ten squared' or 'ten to the power two')}$$

$$1000 = 10 \times 100 \qquad \text{(ten hundreds are one thousand)}$$
$$= 10 \times 10 \times 10$$
$$= 10^3 \qquad \text{('ten cubed' or 'ten to the power three')}$$

$$10\ 000 = 10 \times 1000 \qquad \text{(ten thousands are ten thousand)}$$
$$= 10 \times 10 \times 10 \times 10$$
$$= 10^4 \qquad \text{('ten to the power four')}$$

See how far you can go recording numbers in this way. The table may help you:

millions	hundred thousands	ten thousands	thousands	hundreds	tens	units

Using ^{2} ^{3} ^{4} with numbers, for example 10^2 10^3 10^4—this is called index notation.

The indices show how many tens are multiplied together.

Use this index notation to set out the following examples:

1. $6456 = 6 \times 10^3 + 4 \times 10^2 + 5 \times 10 + 6$
2. $5327 =$
3. $4561 =$
4. $8743 =$
5. $6031 =$

Meeting an Octopus

We know that we generally count using the *denary* scale or *base ten*. And we know that there are other counting systems. Base five is one: the Joloffs of Africa had a primitive quinary system.

In *Let's Discover Mathematics* Book 4 we met a counting octopus. As the octopus has eight tentacles we decided that he would probably count in *base eight*. Let us have another look at our counting octopus!

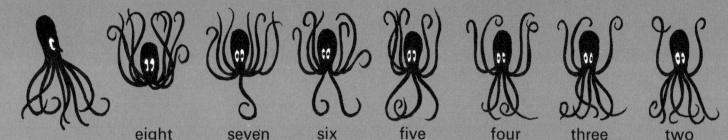

eight   seven   six   five   four   three   two   one

He's counted to eight and has used up all his tentacles. He needs help if he is to count on.

1 He calls to his friend.

2 He touches his friend.

3 His friend puts one of his tentacles up to stand for the eight counted and our octopus begins to count again.

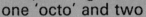

Now copy these drawings, making sure each one has the correct number of tentacles.

one 'octo' and two

one 'octo' and three

one 'octo' and four

one 'octo' and five

More about Tentacles

Copy and complete these drawings:

one octo and seven

two octo and three

four octo and six

seven octo and six

Think about the drawings below and then draw what you consider to be correct ones.

1 Should it be 'one octo and eight'?

2 Eight octo and seven. Is this right?

Now we have met the counting octopus we, too, should be able to count in eights. Like the octopus we can use the counting base eight.

To show that we are counting in base 8 we can write a small eight after the numeral, like this: 11_8

For much of our work in earlier *Let's Discover Mathematics* books we used an abacus; we shall find it very useful for working in base eight.

a wire abacus

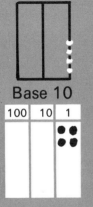

Base 10

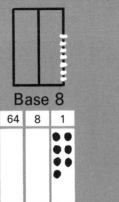

Base 8

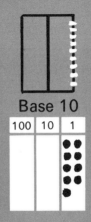

Base 10

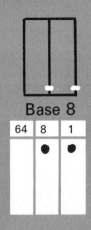

Base 8

Columns ruled on white card and buttons used as counters.

100	10	1
		●● ●●

64	8	1
		●●● ●●● ●●

100	10	1
		●●● ●●● ●●●

64	8	1
	●	●

this page we use drawings of abacus cards ... you have probably already made one for your own use) to help us count in base eight. Like the first column of the denary abacus the right-hand column gives us the units, but each counter in the second column stands for eight.

If we get eight counters in the second column we remove these and replace them with one counter in the third column. We have replaced the set of eight-eights with one counter, $8 \times 8 = 64$. Each counter in the third column stands for 64 just as each counter in the third column of a decimal abacus stands for one hundred (10×10).

Here are some picture numbers on base-eight abacus cards:

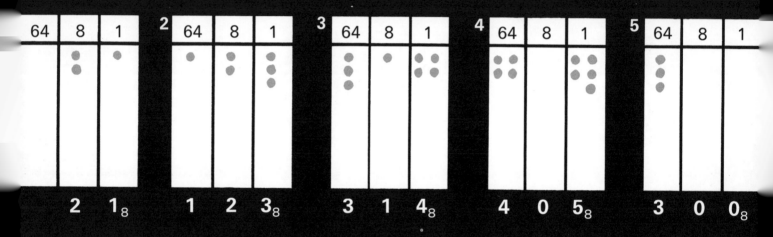

Write the base-eight numerals for these picture numbers:

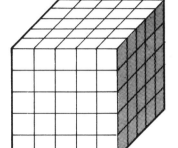

a cube
(sometimes
called a 'block')

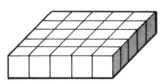

a five layer
(sometimes
called a 'flat')

a five rod
(sometimes
called a 'long')

a unit
cube

Can you work out the 'value' of this base 5 number in the denary scale?

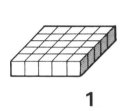

1

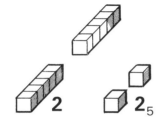

2   **2**$_5$

	denary scale
The cubes represent the units	2
The rods represent the 'fives'	10
The flat represents 5^2 or 5×5	25
$122_5 \rightarrow$	37

Record the following picture numbers in base 5 and in denary. The diagrams are in base 5.

A1

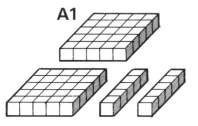

2

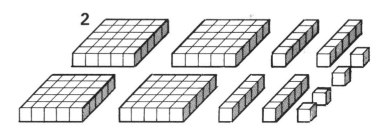

3

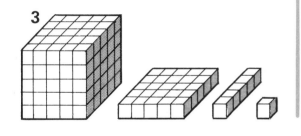

B Record these base 5 numbers in diagram form, or use apparatus; then record in denary.
1 123   **3** 122   **5** 2112
2 213   **4** 444

C Record the following base 5 numbers like this:

1032_5 means
$1 \times 5^3 + 0 \times 5^2 + 3 \times 5 + 2 = \square$

1 1043_5 **3** 1204_5 **5** 1004_5
2 2023_5 **4** 1301_5

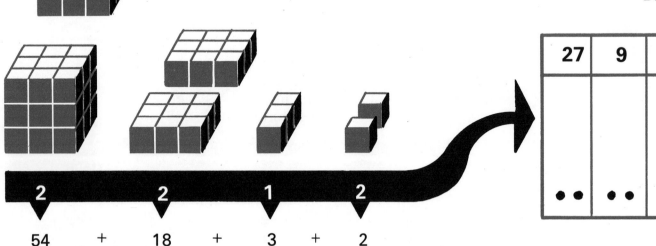

27	9	3	1
••	••	•	••

54 + 18 + 3 + 2

A Change these denary numbers to base 3:

1 13 **3** 26 **5** 66
2 23 **4** 61 **6** 34

B Change these base 3 numbers to denary numbers:

1 21_3 **3** 2121_3 **5** 1010_3
2 2212_3 **4** 2222_3 **6** 2021_3

C If we are keeping the same meaning for our numerals as we would if we were using them in base 10, what numerals would we need to use for:

1 base 5 **3** base 3 **5** base 8
2 base 4 **4** base 6 **6** base 2

D Try these: change them all to the denary scale.

1 76_8 **6** 112_3 **11** 41_6
2 21_8 **7** 122_3 **12** 36_6
3 314_8 **8** 10_5 **13** 123_5
4 405_8 **9** 11_5 **14** 261_7
5 123_4 **10** 13_5 **15** 203_4

Building up a counting table

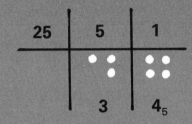

25	5	1
	••	••
		••
	3	4₅

Counters in the right-hand column stand for units, but each counter in the second column stands for five. Five counters in the second column stand for 5×5; these five counters can be replaced by one in the third column.

A Complete this table:

Numerals in base 10	Number of objects	Numeral in base 5	Meaning of base 5 numerals
1	•	1	1
2	• •	2	2
3	• • •	3	3
4	• • • •	4	4
5	• • • • •	10	$1(5)+0$
6	• • • • • •	11	$1(5)+1$
7	• • • • • • •	12	$1(5)+2$
8	• • • • • • • •		
9	• • • • • • • • •		
10	• • • • • • • • • •		
11	• • • • • • • • • • •		
12	• • • • • • • • • • • •		

the same as in the denary scale

B Complete this addition table:

```
base 5   + | 0 1 2 3 4
           0 | 0 1 2 3 4
           1 |
           2 |
           3 |
           4 |
```

C Complete this multiplication table:

```
base 5   × | 0 1 2 3 4
           0 | 0 0 0 0 0
           1 |
           2 |
           3 |
           4 |
```

D Make up addition and multiplication tables for base 10 and base 8.

Number patterns

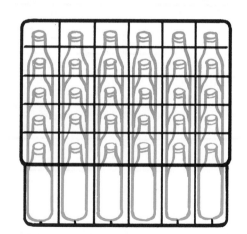

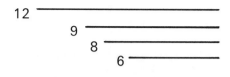

Strings of proportionate lengths 12, 9, 8 and 6 give the following notes when plucked: doh, fah, soh and doh

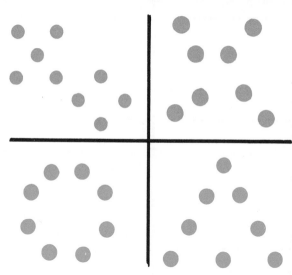

Make up a booklet of your own about 'Number patterns'. Use this page as 'starters' for your own investigations. When you feel you have made a good start, look at page 57 for examples of other people's investigations. They may help you to think up more of your own.

What do you notice?

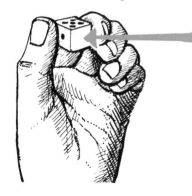

What will this number be?

$4 + \triangle = \square$

Dominoes, cards and dice have special patterns of numbers so that we soon learn to recognise them—without counting.

Use your dice to make up the set of counting numbers. Record the number for each throw.

Try this for other faces of the dice. Does it always happen?

$\{1, 2, 3 \ldots\}$ natural numbers

What does this sentence mean? $2 \in \{\text{natural numbers}\}$
Record the sentence in words.

What pattern does this show? $2 \in \{\text{even numbers}\}$

1
3
6
10
15

Can you see a pattern?
Can you discover a quick way of finding the total number of oranges in the pyramid?

Choose a number of pebbles and see how many different patterns you can make. Record your discoveries.

Patterns

$$1 = 1$$
$$1+1 = 2$$
$$1+1+1 = 3$$
$$1+1+1+1 = 4$$
$$1+1+1+1+1 = 5$$
$$1+1+1+1+1+1 = 6$$
$$1+1+1+1+1+1+1 = 7$$
$$1+1+1+1+1+1+1+1 = 8$$
$$1+1+1+1+1+1+1+1+1 = 9$$

We have used this addition pattern to give us the set of whole or *natural numbers*. They are sometimes called the counting numbers.

$\{1, 2, 3 \ldots\}$ natural numbers

You will need 25 counters for the work on this page.

A rectangular number can be arranged in a number of equal rows and every rectangular number has two or more factors. 0 and 1 are normally included in the pattern of rectangular numbers.

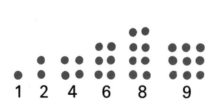

1   2   4   6   8   9

Make your own patterns for rectangular numbers and continue the pattern to 25.

Some of the rectangular numbers can be arranged as square numbers:

•	1	=	1 × 1
	4	=	2 × 2
	9	=	3 × 3
	16	=	4 × 4
	25	=	5 × 5

A square number is one which can be recorded as the product of two equal factors.

Complete this sentence:
$\{\text{square numbers}\} = \{0, 1, 2 \ldots\}$

What do you notice? What can you say about the difference between two consecutive square numbers?

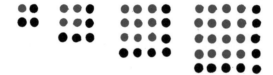

Try drawing the next pattern.

Patterns from numbers

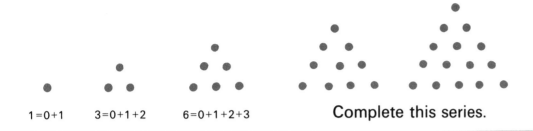

1=0+1   3=0+1+2   6=0+1+2+3

Complete this series.

What do you notice about the number of counters in the longest line (or base) of the triangle and the number of rows in the triangle? Is it always the same?

Each triangular number is the sum of all the whole numbers from 1 up to the number of lines in the triangle. Check this by completing the following pattern:

1 = **1**

1 + 2 = **3**

1 + 2 + 3 = **6**

1 + 2 + 3 + 4 = **10**

1 + 2 + 3 + 4 + 5 = **15**

1 + 2 + 3 + 4 + 5 + 6 + 7 + 8 + 9 + 10 = **55**

{1, 3, 5 . . .} set of triangular numbers

Use your knowledge of set language to record other facts about triangular numbers.

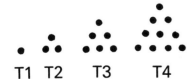

T1 T2   T3   T4

What do T3 and T4 mean in this table?

Moving two triangles together—the result is a rectangle.

$$\begin{matrix} \bullet & \bullet & \bullet & \bullet & \bullet & 1 \\ \bullet & \bullet & \bullet & \bullet & \bullet & 2 \\ \bullet & \bullet & \bullet & \bullet & \bullet & 3 \\ \bullet & \bullet & \bullet & \bullet & \bullet & 4 \end{matrix}$$

4   3   2   1

The number of *lines in the rectangle* is the same as the number of *lines in each triangle.*

If you multiply the number of lines in the triangle by the next higher number, you will find the number of counters in the rectangle.

The rectangle has twice as many counters as each triangle, so we divide the product by 2 to obtain the number of counters in the triangle.

For T4 $\dfrac{4 \times 5}{2} = 10$

For T10 $\dfrac{10 \times 11}{2} = 55$

Try T25, T15, T5 and T100

59

and 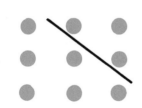 numbers

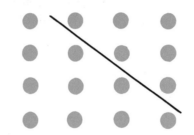

$$T1 + T2 = \ 1 + \ 3 = \ 4 = 2^2$$
$$T2 + T3 = \ 3 + \ 6 = \ 9 = 3^2$$
$$T3 + T4 = \ 6 + 10 = 16 = 4^2$$
$$T4 + T5 = 10 + 15 = 25 = 5^2$$

Complete this table. Decide on a reasonable upper limit!

What is the connection between square and triangular numbers?

Complete this table (again decide on a reasonable upper limit):

0	1	3	6		triangular numbers
0	1	3	6	10	triangular numbers
0	1	4	9	16	Add each column

(0 is usually included in the table of triangular numbers)

$\left\{ 0, \ 1, \ 4, \ 9, \ 16 \ . \ . \ . \right\}$ set of square numbers

Try this:

Eight times any triangular number, and add 1:

$T1 = 1 \quad 8 \times 1 = 8 \ + 1 = 9 = 3^2$ Complete this table
$T2 = 3 \quad 8 \times 3 =$
$T3 = 6 \quad 8 \times 6 =$
$T4$
$T5$
$T6$
$T7$

Do you notice a pattern of odd numbers—yet again?

Pascal's Triangle

```
            1

         1     1

      1     2     1

   1     3     3     1

1     4     6     4     1

1  5  10  10  5  1

1  6  15  20  15  6  1
```

If you toss 1 coin, the chance of getting heads is 1 out of 2.	1 coin
If you toss 2 coins, the chance of getting 2 heads is 1 out of 4; of getting 1 head and 1 tail, 2 out of 4; of getting 2 tails, 1 out of 4.	2 coins
	3 coins
	4 coins
	5 coins
In six tosses the chance of getting all heads or all tails is 1 in 64; 5 heads and 1 tail (or the reverse) 6 out of 64; 4 heads and 2 tails (or the reverse) 15 out of 64; 3 and 3, 20 out of 64.	6 coins

The first number in a line shows the chance of getting all heads. The next number in each line shows the chance of getting all but one head (or tail) and so on down the line.

Can you work out the pattern of probability so as to complete the table?

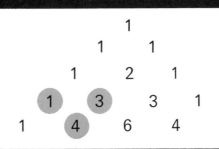

Making Pascal's Triangle

Can you discover how the Pascal Triangle can be formed? Continue the pattern.

Number patterns

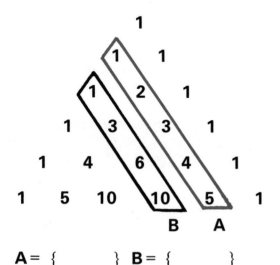

The sum of the numbers in the row is:

```
                    1              →    1
                 1     1           →    2 = 2¹
              1     2     1        →    4 = 2²
           1     3     3     1     →    8 = 2³
        1     4     6     4     1  →   16 = 2⁴
     1    5    10    10    5    1  →   32 = 2⁵
  1    □    15    □    □    □    1 →   64 = 2⁶
1   □   21   □    □    □    □   1 → 128 = 2⁷
```

$$1 \to 1$$
$$2 = 2^1$$
$$4 = 2^2$$
$$8 = 2^3$$
$$16 = 2^4$$
$$32 = 2^5$$
$$64 = 2^6$$
$$128 = 2^7$$

Complete the pattern in the Pascal Triangle and the tabulation of the sum of numbers in each row.

What do you notice when you add the natural numbers in each row?

What do you notice about the numbers in **A** and **B**?

```
            1
         1     1
       1    2     1
     1    3    3    1
   1    4    6    4    1
 1    5   10   10    5    1
              B    A
```

A = {   }   **B** = {   }

Using odd numbers

1 Complete the pattern:

```
             1
          3     5
       7     9    11
    13   15    17    19
 21   □    □    □    □
```

2 Complete the tabulation:

(the sum of the numbers in the row is)

$$1 = 1$$
$$8 = 2^3$$
$$27 = 3^3$$
$$\square = \triangle^{\triangle}$$
$$\square = \triangle^{\triangle}$$

Prime numbers

1	2	3	4	5	6	7	8	9	10
11	12	13	14	15	16	17	18	19	20
21	22	23	24	25	26	27	28	29	30
31									
41									
51									60
61									
71									
81									
91								99	100

Finding the prime numbers

Any numbers except the prime numbers can be thought of as the product of two or more factors.

The ancient method for sifting out the prime numbers is known as the Sieve of Eratosthenes, after the Greek who worked out the method.

To find the prime numbers up to 100 we use the '100 square'. Make up your own 1–100 Number Square, numbering each square.

Using
the
Sieve

The first prime number is generally considered to be 1. Leave this square untouched.

The next number is 2 which you again leave but cross out every second number after 2. These are the *even* numbers which are divisible by 2 and are not prime— other than 2 itself.

The next number is 3 which you leave, and cross out every third number after 3. Repeat this process for 4, 5, 6, 7, 8, 9 and 10.

1 Can you see why this will be enough to ensure that all the uncrossed numbers left will be primes, provided that we work with a 100 square?

2 Can you work out what number we would need to make our stopping point for crossing out, when looking for prime numbers less than 200?

Working with numbers

A whole number greater than 1 which is not a prime number is called a *composite* number.

Using prime numbers we can build all composite numbers by multiplication.

Make up a table using the primes 2, 3, 5, 7 . . .

Using prime numbers

Using one prime factor	2	3
Using two prime factors	$2 \times 3 = 6$ $2 \times 5 = 10$	$3 \times 5 = 15$ $3 \times 7 = 21$
Using three prime factors	$2 \times 3 \times 5 = 30$ $2 \times 5 \times 7 = 70$	

	2	3	5	7
Using one prime factor				
Using two prime factors				
Using three prime factors				

Reversing the process

Instead of starting with prime numbers we can start with a composite number and break it down into its prime factors.

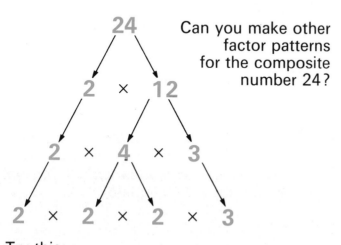

Can you make other factor patterns for the composite number 24?

Try this:

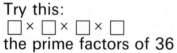

$\square \times \square \times \square \times \square$
the prime factors of 36

Making the pattern with rods or diagrams:

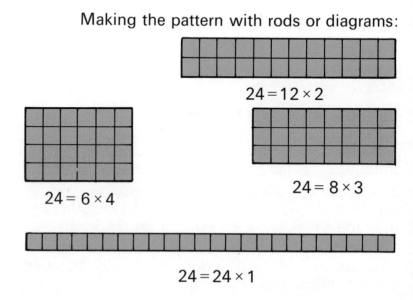

$24 = 12 \times 2$

$24 = 6 \times 4$

$24 = 8 \times 3$

$24 = 24 \times 1$

1	2	3	4	5	6	7	8	9	10	11	12
2											
3											
4											
5											
6											
7											
8											
9											
10											
11											
12											

What pattern is this?
What pattern of numbers is shown by the centre diagonal?
What do you notice about the pattern on either side of the diagonal? Is there a balance?
Think about this: $5 \times 6 = 6 \times 5$

What pattern is this?

1	2	3	4	5	6	7	8	9	10
11	12	13	14	15	16	17	18	19	20
21	22	23	24	25	26	27	28	29	30
31	32	33	34	35	36	37	38	39	40
41	42	43	44	45	46	47	48	49	50
51	52	53	54	55	56	57	58	59	60
61	62	63	64	65	66	67	68	69	70
71	72	73	74	75	76	77	78	79	80
81	82	83	84	85	86	87	88	89	90
91	92	93	94	95	96	97	98	99	100

Make up as many patterns as possible using multiplication and Number Squares

Other square patterns:
Multiples of 3

1	2	3	4	5	6	7	8	9	10	11	12
13	14	15	16	17	18	19	20	21	22	23	24
25	26	27	28	29	30	31	32	33	34	35	36
37	38	39	40	41	42	43	44	45	46	47	48
49	50	51	52	53	54	55	56	57	58	59	60
61	62	63	64	65	66	67	68	69	70	71	72
73	74	75	76	77	78	79	80	81	82	83	84
85	86	87	88	89	90	91	92	93	94	95	96
97	98	99	100	101	102	103	104	105	106	107	108
109	110	111	112	113	114	115	116	117	118	119	120
121	122	123	124	125	126	127	128	129	130	131	132
133	134	135	136	137	138	139	140	141	142	143	144

Another pattern

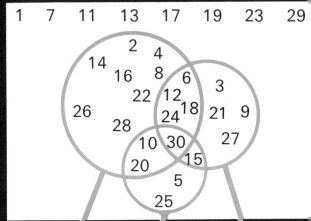

1　7　11　13　17　19　23　29

Multiples of 2
Multiples of 5
Multiples of 3

This Venn diagram shows the multiples of 2, 3 and 5.

Use this idea to show:
1 the multiples of 2 and 3
2 the multiples of 2, 3 and 4
3 the multiples of 3, 4 and 5

Growing squares

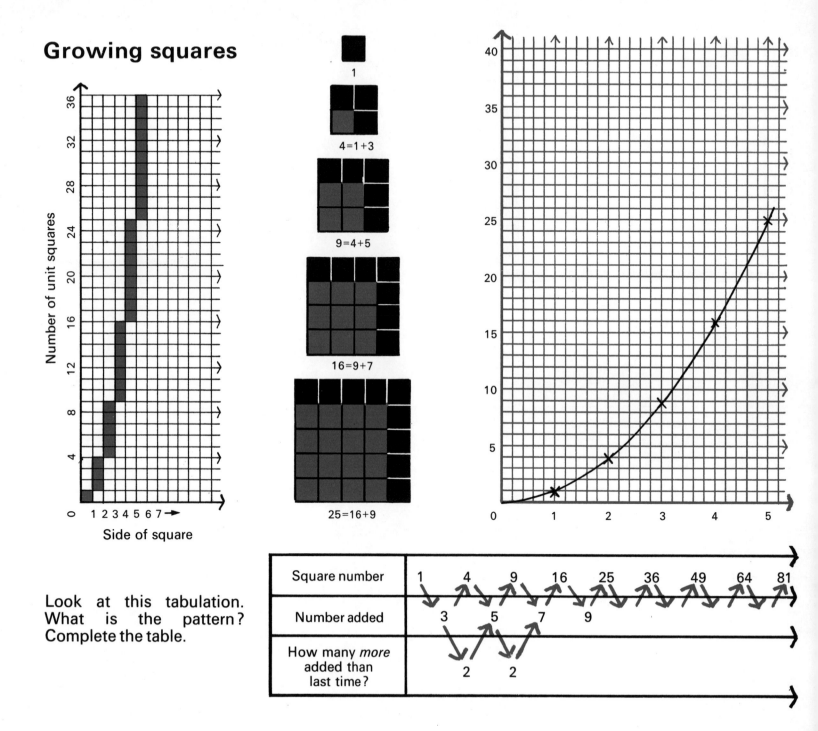

Number of unit squares

Side of square

1

4 = 1 + 3

9 = 4 + 5

16 = 9 + 7

25 = 16 + 9

Look at this tabulation. What is the pattern? Complete the table.

Square number	1	4	9	16	25	36	49	64	81
Number added		3	5	7	9				
How many *more* added than last time?		2	2						

Making staircases

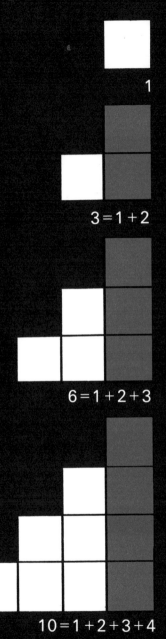

1

3 = 1 + 2

6 = 1 + 2 + 3

10 = 1 + 2 + 3 + 4

What pattern of numbers does this show?

Investigating numbers

N = {natural numbers}
P = {prime numbers}
E = {even numbers}
O = {odd numbers}
S = {square numbers}
T = {triangular numbers}
U = the universal set

Use your knowledge of sets to record—using sets and Venn diagrams—many of your investigations of numbers and their properties.

A Here is one example:

U = N

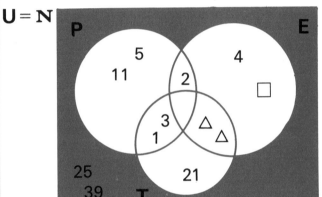

What does this Venn diagram show? Complete the diagram by filling in □ and △ spaces.
Shade in any empty section.

B To which sets do these numbers belong?

1	3	**6**	1
2	9	**7**	55
3	25	**8**	21
4	10	**9**	13
5	16	**10**	4

C Sort the numbers 1–50 into the sets.

D Some numbers are elements of more than one set of multiples; for example, 12 is an element of the set of multiples 2 and 3.

We record this in set language:
12 ∈ {2, 4, 6, 8, 10, 12, 14 ...}
12 ∈ {3, 6, 9, 12, 15, 18 ... }

Is 12 an element of the set of any other multiples? If so, record the sets.

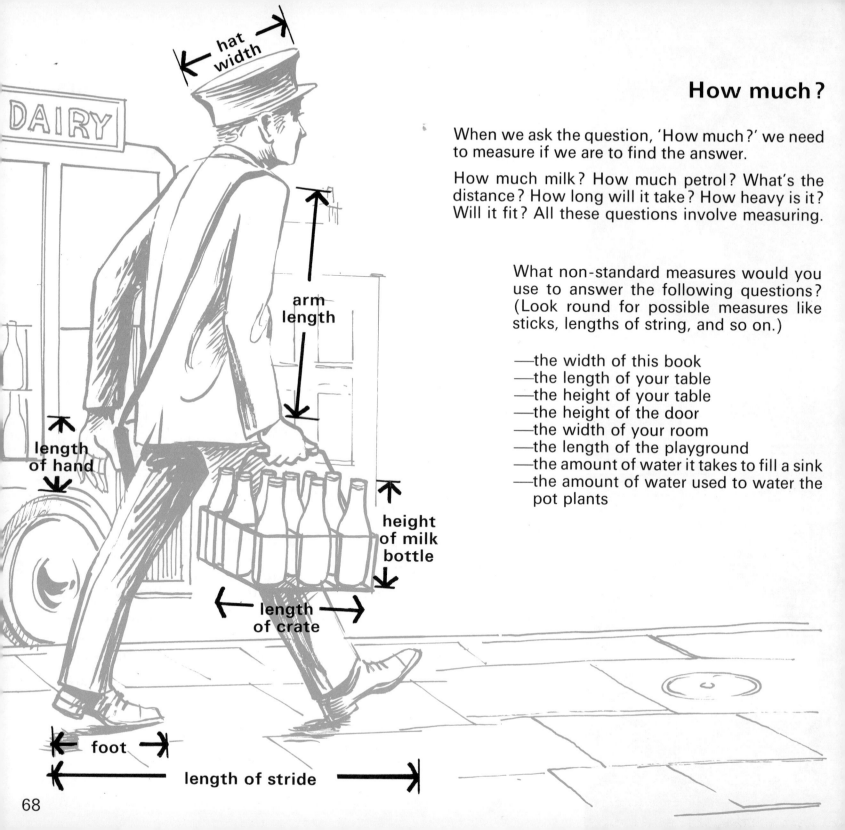

How much?

When we ask the question, 'How much?' we need to measure if we are to find the answer.

How much milk? How much petrol? What's the distance? How long will it take? How heavy is it? Will it fit? All these questions involve measuring.

What non-standard measures would you use to answer the following questions? (Look round for possible measures like sticks, lengths of string, and so on.)

—the width of this book
—the length of your table
—the height of your table
—the height of the door
—the width of your room
—the length of the playground
—the amount of water it takes to fill a sink
—the amount of water used to water the pot plants

Measuring length

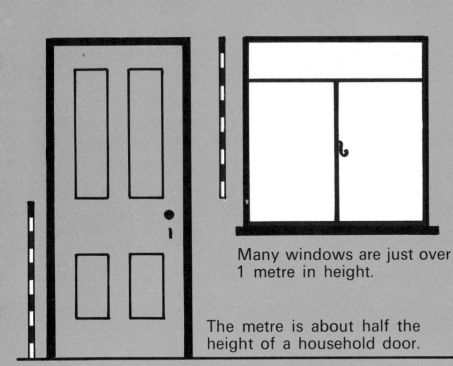

The metre, which is used for measuring length, is the basis of the metric system.

The metre is one of the six international basic units of measurement that are called SI units. This is the abbreviation for Système International d'Unités (see page 96).

Many windows are just over 1 metre in height.

The metre is about half the height of a household door.

A normal table is a little less than three quarters of a metre in height.

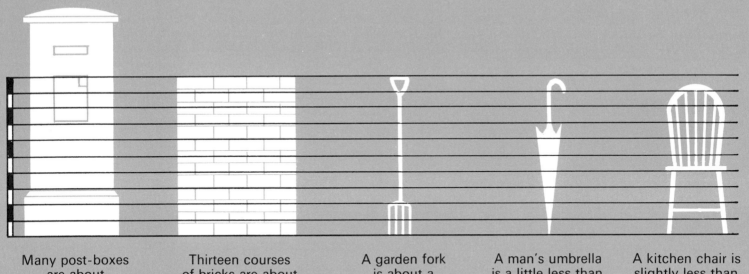

Many post-boxes are about 1½ metres high.

Thirteen courses of bricks are about a metre in height.

A garden fork is about a metre in length.

A man's umbrella is a little less than a metre long.

A kitchen chair is slightly less than a metre in height.

See how many objects you can find that ≙ metre in length.
Try estimating the length of various objects in metres.

Find the lengths of various cars, the widths of windows and gates. Practise using your idea of a metre length with your estimating.

Fine measurements

```
mm    10   20   30   40   50   60   70   80   90   100  110  120  130  140  150  160  170  180  190  200
```

The metric system of measurement is easy to use because of its constant relationship between the basic units.

Length is measured by the metre which is *multiplied* by 1000 to produce the kilometre (for distances between towns and other road distances) and *divided* by 1000 to give the millimetre for small measurements. The abacus diagram shows you the relationship.

TH 1000	H 100	T 10	U 1	t $\frac{1}{10}$	h $\frac{1}{100}$	th $\frac{1}{1000}$
kilometre (km) 1000	hectometre 100	decametre 10	metre (m) 1	decimetre $\frac{1}{10}$	centimetre (cm) $\frac{1}{100}$	millimetre (mm) $\frac{1}{1000}$

1 Use your millimetre scale to try estimating and measuring, using millimetres. (Coins, stamps, pencils, paper clips and buttons are suitable small objects.)

2 Measure the width of your thumb in millimetres.
3 Check the size (in millimetres) of the standard A2 drawing paper.
4 Try to use the millimetre scale in your experimental work.

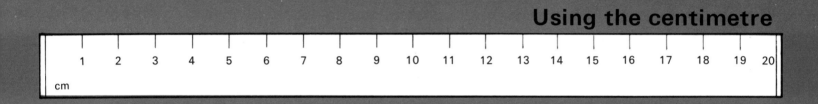

The SI system of units recommends that only sub-multiples and multiples of 1000 are used. Even so, many people will use the centimetre as a convenient unit of measurement.

Use your centimetre scale to measure the lengths of these:

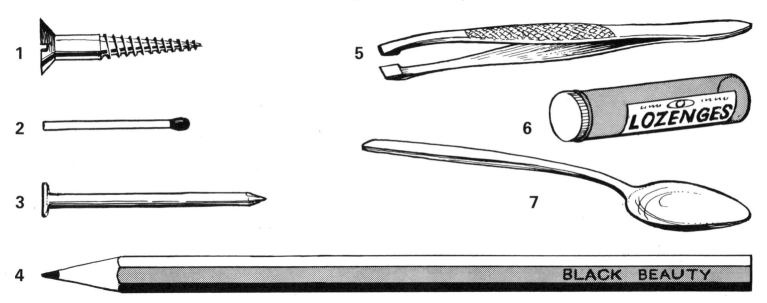

1

2

3

4

5

6

7

Record your estimates of the lengths (in centimetres) of the various objects. Check your estimates by actually measuring. Record your work in a table, like this:

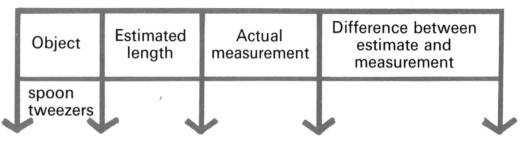

Object	Estimated length	Actual measurement	Difference between estimate and measurement
spoon			
tweezers			

The kilometre

| 5 miles |
| 8 kilometres |

The Imperial system of measurement units includes the inch, the foot, the yard and the mile. The inch is about the same width as a man's thumb; the foot the length of a man's foot and twelve inches in length; the mile is used for measuring distances between towns.

The kilometre is 1000 metres and is the distance that many people can walk in 10 minutes. Try this experiment.

1 Make up a wall chart of the distances (in kilometres and metres) of various distances between your school and places such as the police station, the garage, the church . . . .

2 Make up a list of distances between various towns and London.

3 Using a Continental map, trace out a holiday journey and record the distances in kilometres.

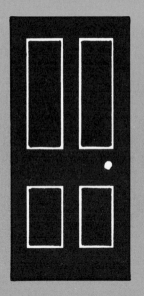

The area of an ordinary household door $\simeq 1\frac{1}{2}$ or $1 \cdot 5\text{m}^2$

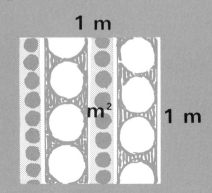

1 m

m² 1 m

How much surface?

A square each side of which is 1 metre has an area of 1 square metre which we record as 1 m².

For the area of small items we use mm².

There is a special unit for measuring land area. It is a hectare which is equivalent to a square measuring 100 metres by 100 metres. The symbol for hectare is ha. It is an area two and a half times as big as the acre.

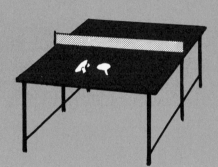

table tennis table 4 m²

floor of a single car garage $\simeq$ 12 m²

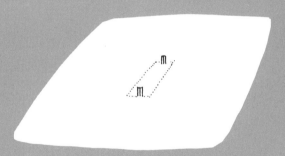

a cricket field measures 1·5 ha

standard postage stamp $\simeq$ 480 mm²

Biddy & Biddy

ESSEX GREAT EASTON

An impressive residence, close to

1·2 hectares (3 Acres)

Things to do:

1 Find the area of various postage stamps (mm²).

2 Find the area of a sheet of newspaper.

3 Build up your own 'aids to estimating' by finding surfaces that $\simeq$ 1 m².

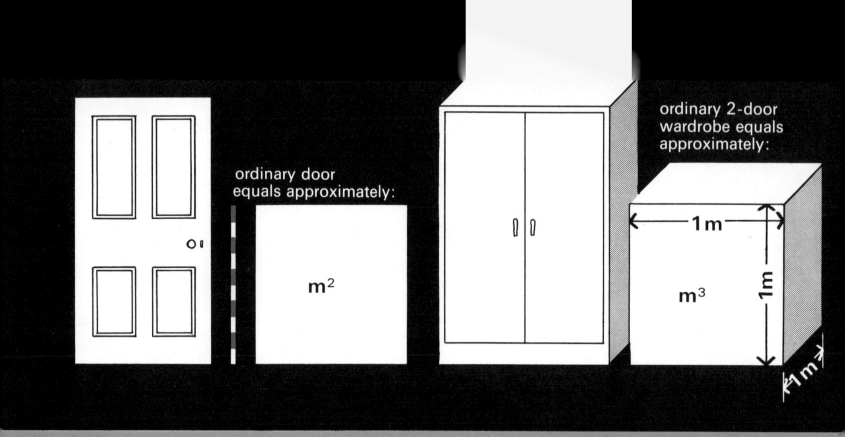

ordinary door
equals approximately:

m^2

ordinary 2-door
wardrobe equals
approximately:

1 m

1 m

m^3

1 m

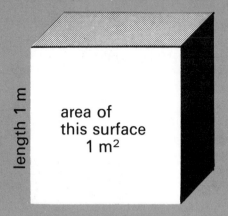

length 1 m

area of
this surface
1 m²

The advantage of the metric system is that not only is the unit of area directly obtained from the unit of length, but also the unit of capacity or volume.

When we convert the metre into a three-dimensional box, each edge of which is 1 metre long, and each surface of which is 1 square metre, we have a box with a volume of 1 cubic metre. We record this as 1 m³. An average household wardrobe is about 1 m³.

Things to do:
Make up a wooden framework to give you 1 m³. Try fitting various objects (and people!) into your cubic metre.

If there is a pile of builders' sand within the school area, you could try measuring out 1 m³ of sand.

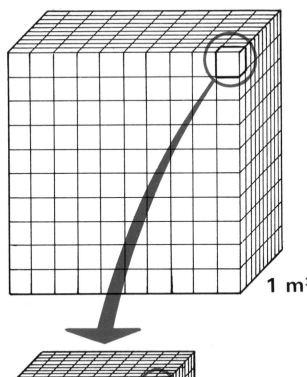

1 m³

Here is a cubic metre (m³) divided into 1000 cubes. Each edge of the smaller cube is one tenth of a metre long (100 millimetres, sometimes called 1 decimetre). Each cube is one thousandth of a cubic metre, or one cubic decimetre, which can be recorded as 1 dm³.

The diagram shows one of the smaller cubes taken away from the 1 m³. This is an important metric measurement, for it has the capacity of 1 litre. The litre is the measure for wine, milk, petrol and other liquids.

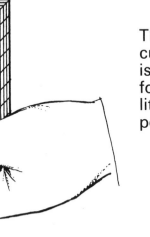

lump of sugar

The litre can be divided into 1000 tiny cubes. Each tiny cube has a volume rather less than a sugar lump.
This thousandth of a litre is called a millilitre (ml). The millilitre is equivalent in volume to one cubic centimetre.

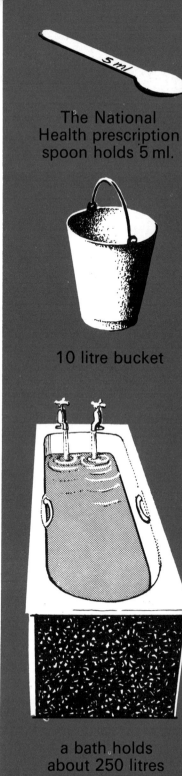

The National Health prescription spoon holds 5 ml.

10 litre bucket

a bath holds about 250 litres

75

How heavy?

The kilogramme is the basic unit of mass.

1 m³

A metre cube when filled with water has a mass of 1000 kilogrammes and this is called a tonne. The tonne is pronounced 'tunny' and its symbol is t.

Things to do:
Use the various metric masses to weigh different objects so that you can begin to estimate the mass of other objects.

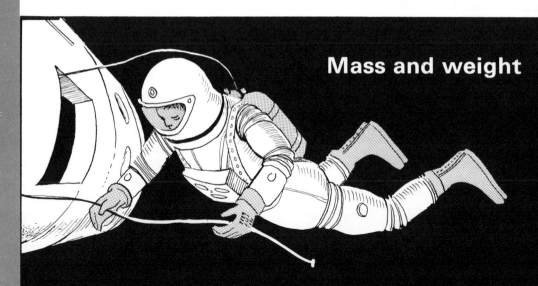

Mass and weight

TV pictures of astronauts show them training for 'weightlessness' in space. We can see that 'weight' is not a static measure, but is dependent on gravitational pull as well as on the mass of a person or object. Mass, on the other hand, is an unchangeable quantity. The difference is not an important one in everyday life on Earth, but if you are interested you could try to find out more about Mass and Weight. With SI units, it is correct to say 'masses' rather than 'weights'.

Making a Magic Square

1

a First write 1 in the middle cell of the right-hand column.

b Move diagonally downward and to the right.

2

2 falls outside the Magic Square but its position corresponds to (is a reflection of) the bottom cell in the first column.

c Place the 2 in its position.

3

d Now that 2 is in position, move diagonally downward again.

4

3 falls outside the Magic Square but the corresponding position (notice the symmetry) is in the top square centre column.

5

6

e We cannot move diagonally downward to write 4 because the numeral 1 is in that square. When this happens, write the numeral in the square to the immediate left of the numeral just written.

7

8

f Moving diagonally downward we have two empty squares which will take numerals 5 and 6.

9

g To move diagonally downward would not give us a square that corresponds to any square in the Magic Square. Look at **e** to discover the 'rule'. Again we write the numeral to the left of the numeral just written.

10

h See **d** for explanation.

11

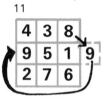

i The complete chart for the moves looks like this:

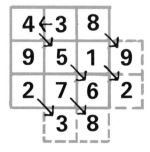

B Now try this one on your own:

		$\frac{1}{3}$

Triangles and crosses

Using the numerals 1–9:

Can you discover what is happening?

	6	7	
2	11	4	9
3	1	10	12
	8	5	

Try to make other number puzzles of your own.

Patterns

Can you see how this pattern is formed?

1 1 2 3 5 8 13 21 34 . . .

If you need a clue:

1 1 2 **3 5 8** 13 and 1 1 2 3 5 8 **13 21 34**

3+5=8   13+21=34

Find the next five numbers in the sequence.   What can you say about the pattern?

Any number in this sequence is the sum of any pair of numbers immediately. . . .
A pair of numbers when added together will give. . . .

This number sequence is named after Leonardo Fibonacci who was born in 1175. He discovered this sequence in AD 1202 when trying to solve a problem connected with the breeding of rabbits.

Studying bees   (F—female   M—male)

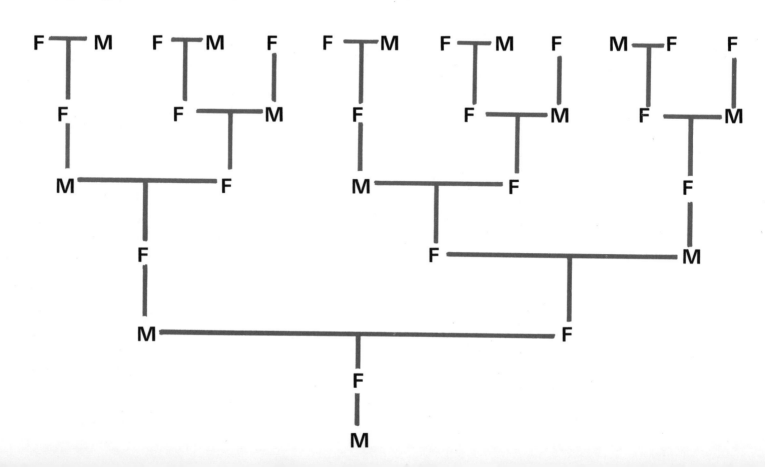

Bees

Queen   Drone   Worker

The fertilised eggs laid by the Queen Bee hatch into female bees. The females are either Workers or Queens. Male bees—called Drones—only hatch from unfertilised eggs. When you trace the family tree of a drone, you will see that the number of ancestors in any one generation is a Fibonacci number.

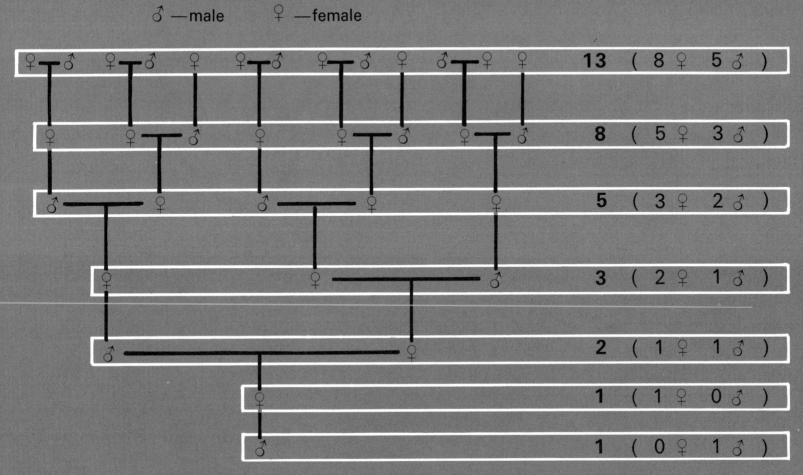

♂ —male   ♀ —female

Looking at plants

one one two three five eight thirteen twenty-one thirty-four . . .
Yes, it is the Fibonacci sequence again.

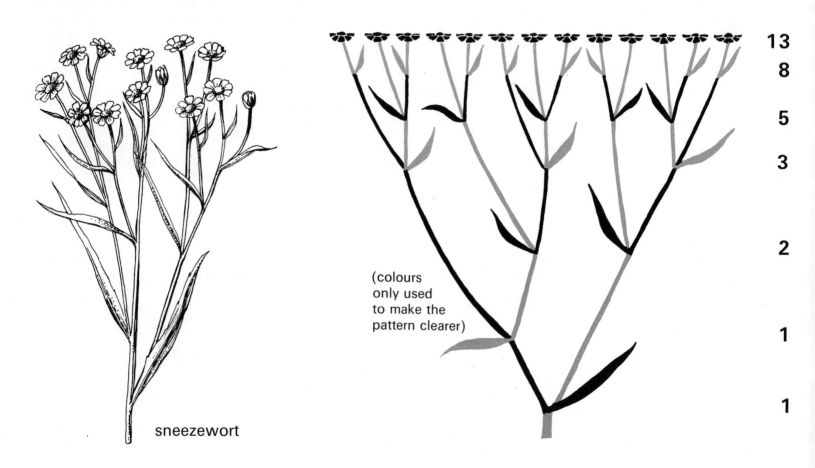

13
8
5
3
2
1
1

(colours only used to make the pattern clearer)

sneezewort

A new shoot generally grows out at the point where the leaf grows from the main stem of the plant. Further leaves and branch shoots grow at the next stage and these are the sum of those from the main and branch stems.

In nature, variations in temperature, sunlight, etc. affect the pattern but the diagram of the sneezewort shows a completely normal growth pattern.

Look again at the 'family tree' of the bee on page 78. What do you notice? Write about your discoveries.

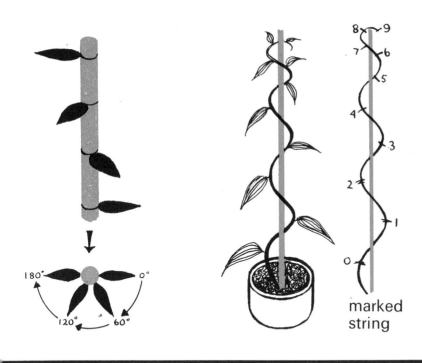

The majority of plants have leaves and shoots that develop round the main stem. If one leaf is on the north side of the plant the next will be 60° round from the north, the next 120° round from the north, climbing upwards in a spiral form.

Why do you think leaves are arranged in this spiral form?

Try arranging a piece of string in a spiral, touching each leaf. You should be able to see how many times it goes round between opposite leaves or buds.

marked string

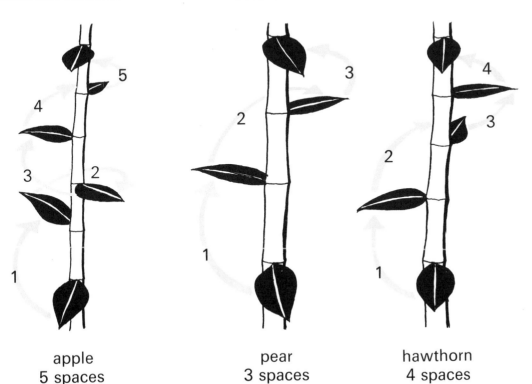

All plants do not have the same leaf pattern.

apple: 5 spaces of 72° each
pear: 3 spaces of 120° each
hawthorn: 4 spaces of 90° each

apple
5 spaces

pear
3 spaces

hawthorn
4 spaces

Fibonacci Ratios

holly $\frac{3}{8}$ (in 3 full turns there are 8 leaves)

The numerator is the number of turns round the stem. The denominator is the number of leaves in the cycle before another leaf grows *directly* above any leaf previously counted.

The amount of turning from one leaf to the next is a fraction of a complete turn or circle round the stem.

$\frac{3}{8}$ **spiral**

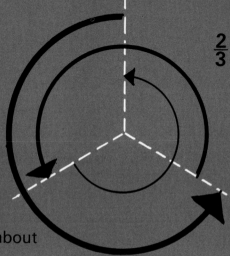

$\frac{2}{3}$

What do you notice about this fraction?

Investigate this idea for recording leaf growth with other plants.

Looking at flowers

two
three
five
eight
thirteen
twenty-one
thirty-four
fifty-five
eighty-nine

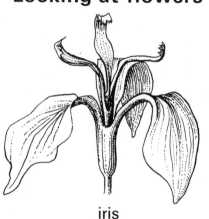

iris

lesser celandine

double delphinium

More flowers

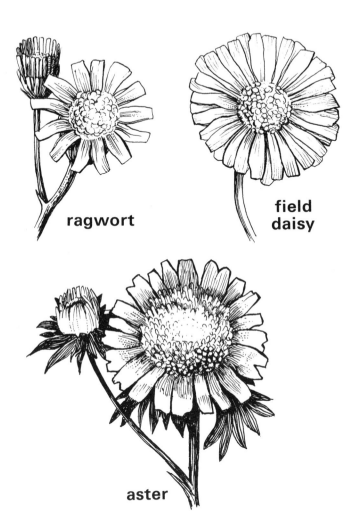

ragwort

field daisy

aster

The daisy family contains flowers that have tightly packed florets in the centre of each head. The outer ring of ray florets can be easily counted and the average totals follow the Fibonacci sequence.

An investigation

Make a collection of daisies from a lawn and count the number of florets or 'petals' on each head. Make a graph of your results. Is it reasonable to select one of the Fibonacci series as a general number for the total of daisy florets? What do you notice about the distribution of totals either side of the number? How do you explain your results?

Count five scales along the spiral in one direction. How many scales correspond to this when you count in the opposite direction? What do you notice about the numbers?

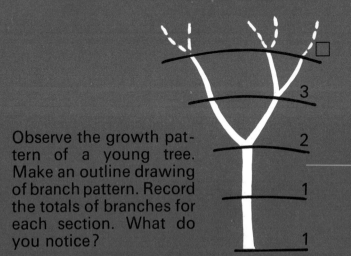

Observe the growth pattern of a young tree. Make an outline drawing of branch pattern. Record the totals of branches for each section. What do you notice?

Plant survey

Choose an interesting area of uneven ground by your school or in your garden at home and make a scale plan of the chosen plot. Represent the various plants in the plot by symbols.

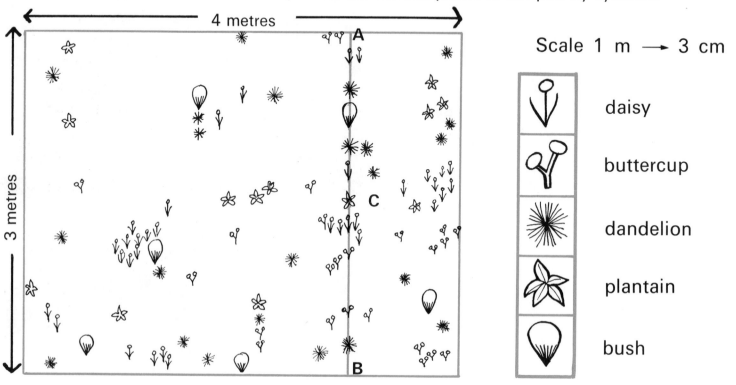

4 metres

3 metres

A

B

C

Scale 1 m ⟶ 3 cm

daisy

buttercup

dandelion

plantain

bush

A more accurate mapping of a small section of your plot can be found by stretching a length of string across the plot. Drive in poles at **A**, **B** and **C**.

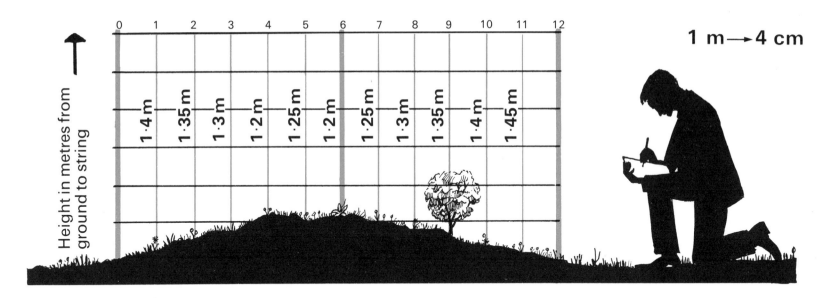

1 m ⟶ 4 cm

Measure the height above the ground of all the points 0 to 12 and record them on a graph. At each interval drop a weighted line and record the plant which is growing immediately below. This will give you a profile of this section of the ground.

Record each position on the graph using the same symbols that you used for the plot map to represent the different plants. Compare the distribution of plants on your plant profile with those made by other children in your class.

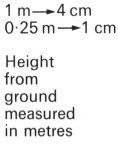

1 m ⟶ 4 cm
0·25 m ⟶ 1 cm

Height from ground measured in metres

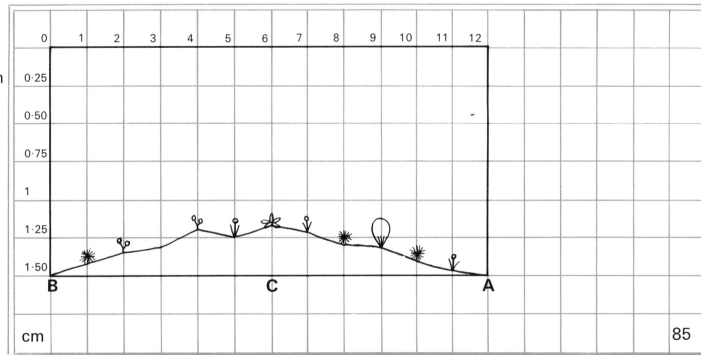

cm

Yellow and green peas

The science of genetics is the study of the ways in which the characteristics of parents are passed to their children. Plants, insects, and small animals like rats and mice, are studied and, of course, Man is studied too. When you ask, 'Where did you get your brown eyes from?' the question really needs a scientific answer!

Parents' characteristics are passed on through germ cells which are either male or female. Each germ cell has a nucleus and within this can be found chromosomes. The chromosomes contain the genes which determine such things as the colour of the eyes. At fertilisation, when the germ cells divide, the chromosomes divide in two, one half going to each new cell. This means that the new plant or animal has the same number of chromosomes as its parents.

An Austrian monk, called Gregor Mendel, carried out experiments in crossing sweet pea plants by fertilising the seed of one plant with the pollen from another. He found that if he mated a pea with yellow seed leaves with a pea that had green seed leaves, all the following generation had yellow seed leaves. The gene carrying 'yellowness' in the seed leaves of peas is, therefore, called *dominant* and the gene carrying green is called *recessive*.

When two of the first generation hybrids mated, Mendel found that he got peas in the ratio of 3 with yellow seed leaves to 1 with green. He actually counted 6022 yellow and 2001 green, which is approximately equal to a 3:1 ratio.

It is very easy to represent Mendelian inheritance by drawing a diagram to show what happens when yellow and green seed leaved peas are mated together.

The genes on the chromosomes are represented by **(YY)** for the dominant yellow colour, and **(gg)** for the recessive green colour.

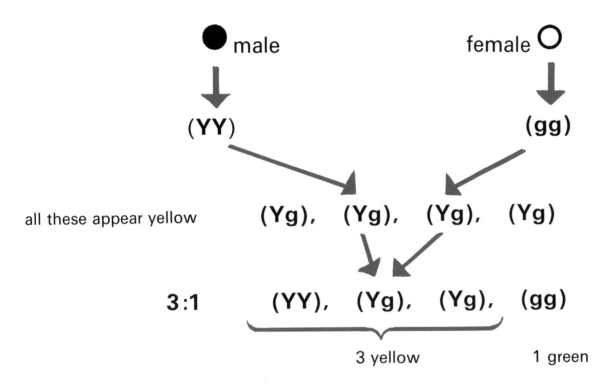

● male

female ○

(YY)

(gg)

all these appear yellow

(Yg),   (Yg),   (Yg),   (Yg)

3:1

(YY),   (Yg),   (Yg),   (gg)

3 yellow

1 green

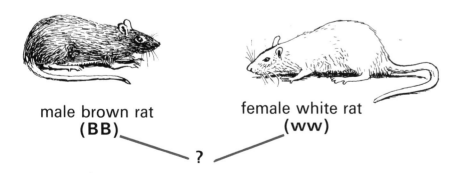

male brown rat
(BB)

female white rat
(ww)

?

Brown and white rats

A pure brown male rat mated with a pure white female rat. The brown gene is dominant. Try to work out the colour proportions (the ratio) for first and second generation babies.

Experimenting

You will need several hundred counters, half of one colour and half of another. Let us take yellow and green counters as an example. Place half the yellow and half the green counters in one box. Place the remaining halves in a second box.

With your eyes closed, select one counter from each box and arrange them as a pair. This corresponds to fertilisation. You may get

        2 yellow counters
or 1 yellow 1 green
or 2 green

Record your results. When you have made about a hundred 'fertilisations', work out your results as a ratio in terms of pure yellow, pure green and yellow and green mixtures. Check your results with those of your friends.

Enlarging

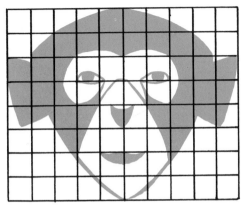

One way of enlarging or reducing a picture is to use a squared grid. In the diagram the measurements of the first picture are doubled. What remains the same in the picture? What changes?

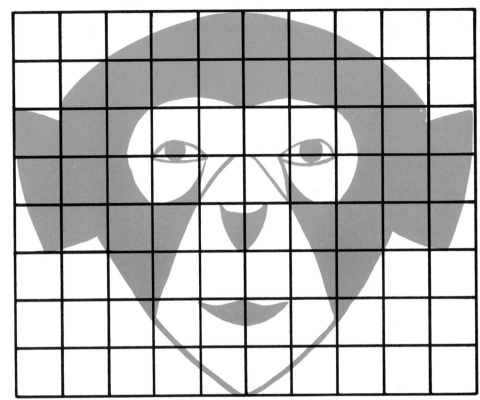

twice the size grid

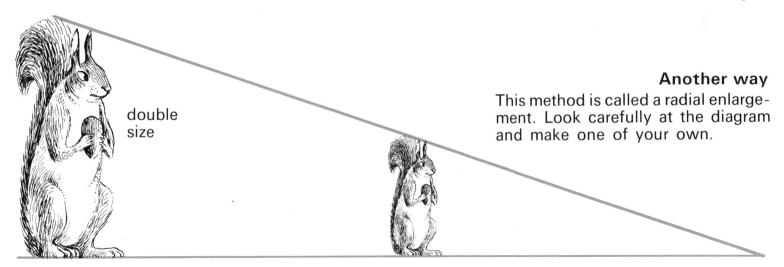

double size

Another way
This method is called a radial enlargement. Look carefully at the diagram and make one of your own.

Other ways of enlarging

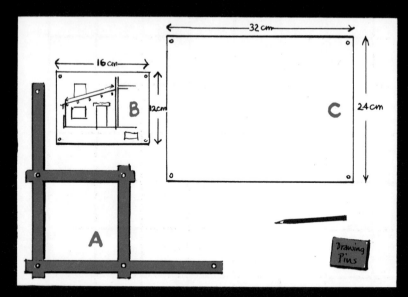

1 A useful way of enlarging a plan or drawing is to use a pantograph (**A**). If the plan (**B**) is to be enlarged to twice the size, place next to it a sheet of paper (**C**) with double the dimensions, and pin both plan and drawing paper firmly to a board.

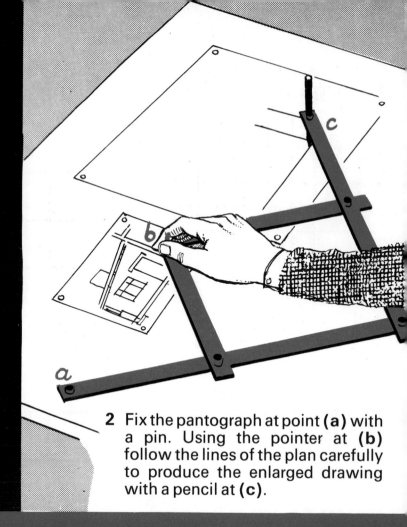

2 Fix the pantograph at point (**a**) with a pin. Using the pointer at (**b**) follow the lines of the plan carefully to produce the enlarged drawing with a pencil at (**c**).

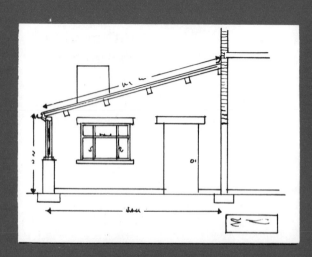

3 The completed enlargement.

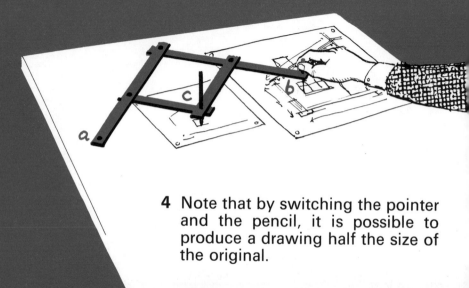

4 Note that by switching the pointer and the pencil, it is possible to produce a drawing half the size of the original.

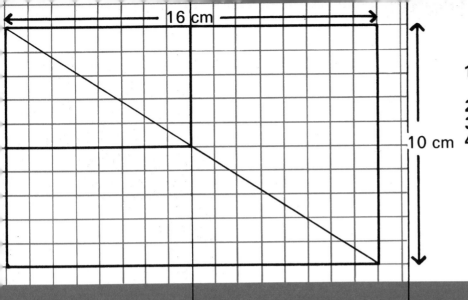

1. On graph paper draw a rectangle with sides 16 cm and 10 cm long.
2. Draw a diagonal.
3. Mark the mid-point of the 16 cm side.
4. Use this point and the diagonal to draw a smaller rectangle.

Sides are in the ratio 1 to 2:

Make up several rectangles of the same shape but different sizes, and cut them out of paper. You can lay one rectangle on top of another.

Draw a diagonal across the rectangles. What do you notice? Are the rectangles of the same size? Are the rectangles of the same shape? Are the rectangles in a set with sides of the same ratio?

Find a photograph that needs to be reduced or enlarged in order to fit exactly between the column lines on this page.

Cut out paper rectangles of your own and use this method to reduce or enlarge them so that they fill an exact number of columns. (This is how photographs are prepared for fitting into a newspaper.)

Circumferences

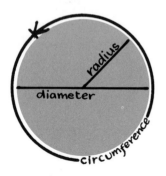

The circumference of any circle is always the same number of times the diameter.

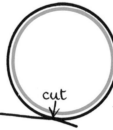

Wind a piece of string round the circumference of a tin lid.

Unwind the string.

Place the lid along the outstretched string. How many times does it fit?

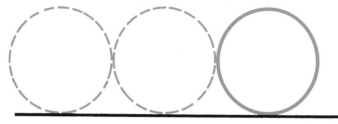

The number of times cannot be written exactly as a fraction or decimal, so we use the Greek letter π (pi) to stand for it. It is almost equal to $3\frac{1}{7}$ or 3·14.

Experimenting with cocktail sticks

There is an interesting way of finding experimentally the value of π by dropping cocktail sticks on a large sheet of paper which has been ruled in divisions; the divisions should be as wide as the cocktail sticks are long. You may be lucky enough to find that the cracks between your floorboards are the correct distance apart but, if not, draw your own 'floorboards' on a sheet of paper.

Drop the cocktail sticks to the floor and record your throw. Count the number of times that a stick falls on a crack (or on one of the lines you have drawn on the paper). The more times you drop the sticks, the more accurate your result will be.

1 Count the number of times you drop the sticks.

2 Count the number of times a stick falls on the crack or line.

3 Double the number of throws and divide this number by the number of times a stick fell on the crack or line.

Drop a stick 200   Stick falls on crack □ times.
Multiply by   2 $400 \div \square = \triangle$ which is an approximate value for π.
―――
400

Can you explain why this experiment gives you an approximate value for π?

Number patterns

A Complete the following number patterns:

1
$$1 = 1$$
$$10 + 1 = 11$$
$$100 + 10 + 1 = 111$$
$$= \square$$
$$= \square$$

2
$$10 - 1 = 9$$
$$100 - 1 = 99$$
$$1000 - 1 = \square$$
$$= \square$$

3
$$9 + 1 = 10$$
$$90 + 10 = 100$$
$$900 + 100 = \square$$
$$= \square$$

4
$$1 \times 9 = 10 - 1$$
$$2 \times 9 = 20 - 2$$
$$3 \times 9 = 30 - 3$$
$$4 \times 9 = \square$$
$$= \square$$
$$= \square$$

5
$$1 \times 8 = 10 - 2$$
$$2 \times 8 = 20 - 4$$
$$3 \times 8 = 30 - 6$$
$$4 \times 8 = \square$$
$$5 \times 8 = \square$$
$$= \square$$

B Making up diagrams

Complete these diagrams:

Make up a pattern of dots to show that the sum of the ordered pairs of numbers is 12.

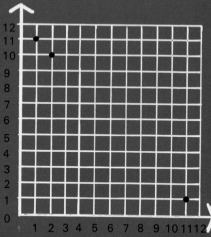

Make up a pattern of dots to show that the first numeral in each ordered pair is two more than the second.

Make up a pattern of dots to show that the product of the ordered pairs is 12.

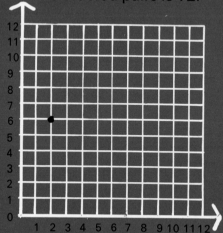

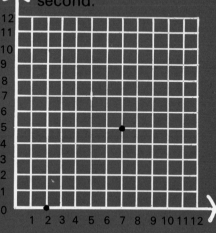

Make up more diagrams of your own.

C Use your Number Line to make various Number Patterns.

94

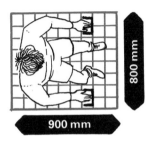

This diagram shows the space required for sitting.

Sizes in building

A When designing buildings, spaces for various activities are worked out in multiples of 100 mm. Make full-size drawings of the diagrams on this page.

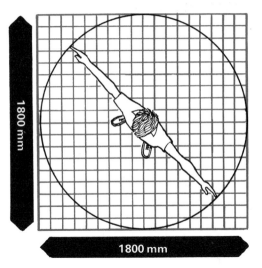

This diagram shows the space required to turn round with arms outstretched.

B Measure the heights in millimetres of furniture, door levers and other items in your classroom. Record your work using a diagram like this:

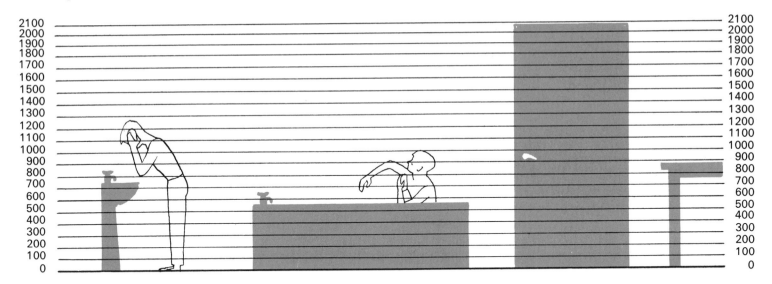

C Make a diagram of the new metric standard size drawing board, 650 mm × 470 mm.

D Cut out a piece of paper to show the size of the new standard A2 drawing paper, 594 mm × 420 mm.

The odd/even pattern is shown.   What do the ▽ and ♀ show?

REFERENCE

SI system The six basic units of measurement are:

for LENGTH   the **metre** (m) ⟶ { with AREA and VOLUME derived from the basic measurement of length

for MASS   the **kilogramme** (kg)

and then for TIME   the **second** (s)

for ELECTRIC CURRENT   the **ampere** (A)

for TEMPERATURE   the **degree Kelvin** (°K) ⟶ { but the measurement used for everyday purposes will be the degree Celsius (°C) which is exactly the same as the degree Centigrade. (Normal body temperature 37°C; sitting room temperature 20°C; boiling water 100°C.)

for LUMINOUS INTENSITY   the **candela** (cd)

you are unlikely to need this measurement

LENGTH	kilometre	km	road distances
	metre	m	**basic unit**
	centimetre	cm	used in schools
	millimetre	mm	for fine measurement
AREA	square kilometre	km²	large area of land
	square metre	m²	**basic unit of area**
	square centimetre	cm²	used in schools
	square millimetre	mm²	for fine measurement
	hectare	ha	area of fields and land
VOLUME	cubic metre	m³	**the basic unit**
	cubic centimetre	cm³	used in schools
	cubic millimetre	mm³	for fine measurement
	litre	l	for liquid measurement $1 \text{ litre} = 0.001 \text{ m}^3 = 1000 \text{ cm}^3$
MASS	kilogramme	kg	**the basic unit**
	gramme	g	for fine measurement
	metric tonne	t	for large quantities $(1 \text{ t} = 1000 \text{ kg})$

Sets You will find these symbols useful:

$=$ is equal to (equals)

$\neq$ is not equal to (does not equal)

$\in$ is an element of/is a member of/belongs to

$\notin$ is not an element of/is not a member of/does not belong to

U   the universal set

N   frequently used as the sign to stand for 'natural numbers'

$\subset$ is the sub-set of/is contained in

$\cap$ intersection: the elements common to both sets

{?}   curly brackets used to enclose the elements of a set or the characteristics of a set e.g. A = { odd numbers }, { 1, 3, 5 . . . }

. . .   three dots to stand for 'and so on'

{ }   or   ∅   stands for an empty set